The Voyages of the

New Zealand Immigration Ship 1860—1864

By Belinda Lansley

*Ancestral Journeys
of New Zealand
Series*

Without the help of the following people this book would not have been possible. Special thanks to:

Stuart Lansley, for editing my work
and Marolyn Diver of Dornie Publishing.

Dornie Publishing Company

Grasmere, Invercargill
www.dorniepublishing.tk

Original text © Belinda Lansley 2013
Images © named individuals, institutions
All rights reserved
ISBN 978-0-473-22999-3

Cover Design by Strawberrymouse Designs

Dedicated to Stuie, Maia, Arielle and Louis

Belinda Lansley

Step Great Great Great Granddaughter of Sarah Winfield Brown, Matron and passenger on the *Gananoque*, 1860

Contents

Introduction

This book covers the history of one of the lesser known ships that ferried new immigrants from Great Britain to New Zealand. As far as I know, this is the first time the whole story of the *Gananoque* has been told in one place, as there are no known books or Internet sites dedicated to the whole story of this ship. I decided to write about it because I had a step great great great grandmother on board who was much loved by the family and her large portraits still remain in the family.

Thanks to the Alexander Turnbull Library for sending me a copy of the Alfred William Craymer diary which is very entertaining and gave me incredible insight into ship life in general.

All sources are referenced carefully at the back of this book. Some sources may have errors. Often in the past people exaggerated or made incorrect entries in the records. Advertisements for ships often made a ship sound better than it really was in order to gain passengers, just as advertisements operate these days. So I have worked with what was available and hope this written record is as accurate as possible.

There were not many accounts from this ship. If anyone has further information on the ship *Gananoque* including ship diaries, family letters or comments in their family history about the journey that you are willing to share, please contact me so it can be added to any future updated editions.

Belinda Lansley

belinda.lansley@yahoo.co.nz

The Ship

Construction of the Ship *Gananoque*

The *Gananoque* was built and registered in 1857 in Quebec, Canada by shipbuilder George Taylor Davie. The registration finished on 12 February 1858 and was transferred to the Port of Liverpool, England.[1] It was a wooden clipper ship with a gross tonnage of 785 tons. George Taylor Davie (1828 – 1907) ran a ship building firm called George T. Davie and sons at Lauzon, Quebec, Canada (now called Levis, Quebec).[2] The firm still exists to this day as MIL Davie Incorporated. They built many wooden ships, moved into steamers and then built 35 warships.[3]

Clipper ship Siam which was built in 1855 and had a tonnage of 743 tons, similar statistics to the Gananoque.[4] No picture has been found for the Gananoque.

The *Gananoque* was built from oak, tamarack and red pine with the dimensions of 158.1 feet length, 32.6 feet breadth and 21.1 feet depth.[5] In 1858 the ship was partly sheathed in felt and yellow metal. It had a weight of 785 tons[5] with a burden of 1400 to 1500 tons, depending on which advertisement you read. The weight of burden was a good guide as to the maximum cargo allowed on board which would make the journey economic, as well as making sure the weight was not exceeded which could cause the ship to sink while at sea. The *Gananoque* was a fairly small ship with some being well over 1000 tons, up to about 4000 tons.[6]

After construction the *Gananoque* was rigged as a ship and advertised as a clipper ship. The name "clipper ship" was a synonym for a merchant ship. They were first created by American ship builders in the 1840s and were extra fast, travelling on average 250 miles per day while other types of ships averaged 150 miles per day. English ship builders started to build them as well. They revolutionised sea transport and were wonderful ships to behold. Clipper ships had at least three masts and square sails and it was this combination that made them so fast and popular in the 19th century.[6]

The Name *Gananoque*

The name of the ship, *Gananoque,* originates from the town Gananoque which is situated on the St Lawrence River in Ontario, Canada, about 500 kms from where the ship was built in Quebec City. The town's name is pronounced "Gan-uh-Nock-way" and is an aboriginal name which means town on two rivers.[7] As well as being situated on the St Lawrence River, it also has the Gananoque River running through it.[8] There is a spelling mistake in the records that hints that the passengers incorrectly pronounced the name "Gan-uh-Noak."[9] To add to the confusion, in Alfred William Craymer's diary, he spells the ship's name "Gananogue" which almost confirms the ship was not pronounced the same as the township in Canada.[10] A couple of Irish families pronounced the name "Gallant Oak" which is different again![11] On first viewing, the author of this book pronounced the name incorrectly too.

Owners of the *Gananoque*

The *Gananoque* was owned by Thomas Bailey and registered in London from 1859 until 1870 in the Lloyd's Register of Shipping. One eighth share in the ship was sold to Archibald Morris who became the ship's captain for two voyages. Willis, Gann & Co. chartered the ship to Lyttelton in 1860 and then Shaw, Savill and Co. of London chartered the boat on three voyages to New Zealand in 1861, 1863 and 1864. After these trips, Lloyd's Register listed the ship as sailing from London to New Zealand with the Commander being D. Ritchie, from 1864 to 1870, however there are no journeys to New Zealand reported in the newspapers after 1864. The *Gananoque* then disappeared from the Register for a few years until 1874 when it reappeared rigged as a barque and owned by W. Johnson, registered in Newcastle.[12] There were other owners of this ship as well.

Willis, Gann & Co. and Shaw, Savill & Co.

Willis, Gann & Co., was one of the leading companies sailing immigrants to New Zealand in the 1850s. In 1858, Robert Shaw and Walter Savill left Willis, Gann & Co., and formed their own company called Shaw, Savill & Co. Shaw, Savill & Co. was to become one of the most well known and respected shipbrokers in the trade. The *Lord Ashley* was the first ship to sail from London, on 28 May 1858. By 1865 the company had fifteen ship journeys running on the New Zealand service and in 1866 this increased to 68 ship voyages.[13] Both Willis, Gann & Co. and Shaw, Savill & Co. ran their own lines of packet ships from Great Britain to New Zealand. A packet ship was originally used for shipping post office mail to the colonies and other places around the world but this meaning was eventually extended to include passengers as well as mail.[14]

In 1854, the provincial governments became responsible for immigration. The Province of Canterbury had the largest immigration scheme of all the provinces, bringing in almost a fifth of all immigrants between 1858 and 1870. Two thirds of all passengers arriving in Canterbury were assisted; generally, half of their fare was paid by the Provincial Government.[15] Willis, Gann & Co. charged £8 for a farm labourer in steerage on the *Clontarf,* between 1855–57[16] but this had increased to £13 10s by 1861, and for some reason then reduced to exactly £13 by 1863 on the *Sebastopol*. In 1863 rival company Messrs. Shaw, Savill secured the contract for carrying emigrants to Otago, the fares being £12 from Glasgow and £13 10s from London.[17] They had the majority of the market at this time. The rates for steerage passengers on the *Gananoque* in 1860 were almost £2 more for an adult in steerage. The reason for this larger price is unknown. Maybe the *Gananoque* was seen as a better quality ship or maybe there was another reason. Rates for passengers in 1860 are as follows:

Single man or woman	£15
Couple	£30
Child	£7 10s
Infant	free

In the 1860 *Gananoque* passenger list there is no mention of the cost for cabin passengers. But for the *Clontarf* from 1855-57, Willis, Gann & Co. were charging £60 for one person in a chief cabin measuring 6 by 7ft, or £40 each for two people. The second cabins were 6ft 9in by 7ft 6 in and for four people this cost £25 per person. Also available were second cabins for married couples measuring 3ft 6in by 7ft 8in at £25 per person.[16] It is likely Shaw, Savill & Co. would have charged higher prices for the *Gananoque* in the 1860s. In an advertisement in *The Times* (London) on 26 November 1862 it appears the fare for travelling on the *Gananoque* was £14 or greater.

The average annual wage for a housemaid in the 1850s–1860s was £11–£14.[18] Therefore the full cost of the journey was a full year's wage. The average annual wage for a farm labourer in England and Wales in 1860 was £30 2s 4d[19], so the full cost of the journey was over a third of their annual wage. We can now see that travel to New Zealand was expensive and what a struggle it was to raise even half the fare. They often had help from family and friends already in the colony and of course the Provincial Government assisted by paying part of the fare.

Life on Board a Clipper Ship

The Willis, Gann & Co. chart from the 1855–1857 period, on page 16, shows the food allocated to the different classes of passengers.[16] The second cabin and steerage passengers were the only ones who received lime juice to keep away the scurvy. Maybe the first class passengers received enough vitamin C from the extra muscatel raisins and preserved carrots that were served to them. In 1863 the *Gananoque* had livestock on board including pigs and sheep, which were slaughtered as needed but Alfred Craymer refused to eat one of the animals because of the poor condition it was in after such a long journey. In 1861 when the *Gananoque* hit a storm, the fowl coups were swept overboard. Fowl were often kept to produce eggs and eventually meat for the passengers.

Water was stored in barrels but became stale and often grew algae or had vermin fall in and die. Food was stored in lidded barrels but if someone left the lid off they would often become contaminated with rat and mice droppings. The bad hygiene often led to dysentery, cholera and many deaths on board. Flour often had weevils. On the *Gananoque* in 1863 Alfred Craymer and his cabin mates could hear the rats squeaking while they slept. One night there were bits of rice found in the soup. It was soon found that the small white things were maggots and they had come from a very large dead and rotting rat which had somehow fallen into the pea soup! Luckily the soup had been well boiled which would have killed any germs.[10]

Married couples' accommodation in steerage: bunks to the left and right; central table; light from the uncovered hatch. (London Illustrated News, 13 April 1844)

Illness was rife on some journeys, especially when steerage passengers were confined below decks during massive storms in the Southern Ocean. The ships were cleaned with vinegar and chloride of lime to remove vomit and make things smell better, while precious water was kept for drinking.

Toileting on ships was not pleasant. Often pieces of rag, soaked in vinegar, were hung on the back of the toilet door. These were used to wipe with and were shared over and over, often leading to dysentery! The sewage was often flushed into the bilge with buckets of water until emptied at port. The bilge was below steerage so the stench was not pleasant. People would be horrified these days but back then hygiene was generally not understood.[20]

The sleeping arrangements were bunk beds for steerage, with single women and single men having their own areas. Families often became separated as most of the time children over the age of 12 were transferred to the single men's or single women's quarters. Bedding was aired in fine weather but often became soaked if water was coming into the ship; this led to influenza and pneumonia outbreaks.[20]

Typical emigrant ship, Duke of Portland 1850. London Illustrated News

Some ships were better managed than others. The low death count on all of the *Gananoque's* journeys suggests good management, and maybe reasonably good weather, but also some good luck that a major outbreak of illness didn't happen during the journeys. The first journey in 1860 to Lyttelton had two deaths, not related to an epidemic, but there were some cases of measles on board. The 1863 journey to Port Chalmers documents no deaths at all which was virtually unheard of in the 1860s.

The Ship

On the more positive side, a ship journey such as this would have been one of life's biggest adventures for the emigrants. They would see and experience things they never dreamed of, including strange sea creatures, new constellations in the skies and a sea voyage which most would never repeat again in their lifetime, culminating in a strange new land at the final port.   At night the passengers entertained each other with music, lectures of the new country and games, made new friends and contacts and looked forward to a brighter future in their new country.

WEEKLY DIETARY SCALE FOR EACH ADULT PASSENGER.

Articles.	Chief Cabin.	Second Cabin.	Steerage.
Preserved Meats	1½ lb.	1½ lb.	1 lb.
Preserved Salmon	½ "	—	—
Assorted Soups	1 "	—	—
Soup and Bouilli	—	½ lb.	—
York Ham	1 "	½ "	—
Tripe	½ "	—	—
Fish	½ "	¼ lb.	—
Prime India Beef	½ "	1 "	1¼ lb.
Irish Mess Pork	1 "	1¼ "	1 "
Biscuit	3 "	4¼ "	3½ "
Flour	4¼ "	4¼ "	3 "
Rice	1 "	1 "	½ "
Barley	¼ "	½ "	—
Peas	½ pint	½ pint	½ pint
Oatmeal	½ "	½ "	1 "
Preserved Milk	¼ "	—	—
Sugar, refined	½ lb.	—	—
Sugar, raw	¼ "	1 lb.	1 lb.
Lime Juice	—	6 oz.	6 oz.
Tea	3 oz.	1½ oz.	1½ oz.
Coffee	5 "	3 "	2 "
Butter	¼ lb.	¼ lb.	6 "
Cheese	¼ "	¼ "	—
Currants	¼ "	¼ "	—
Raisins, Valentia	¼ "	½ "	½ lb.
Raisins, Muscatel	¼ "	—	—
Suet	¼ "	6 oz.	6 oz.
Preserved Carrots	¼ "	—	—
Pickles	¼ pint	¼ pint	¼ pint
Vinegar	¼ "	—	—
Mustard	¼ oz.	¼ oz.	¼ oz.
Pepper	½ "	¼ "	¼ "
Salt	2 "	2 "	2 "
Potatoes, fresh or	3½ lb.	3½ lb.	2 lb.
Preserved ditto	½ "	½ "	½ "
Water	28 quarts	21 quarts	21 quarts

Food chart for Willis, Gann and Co. from 1855-1857

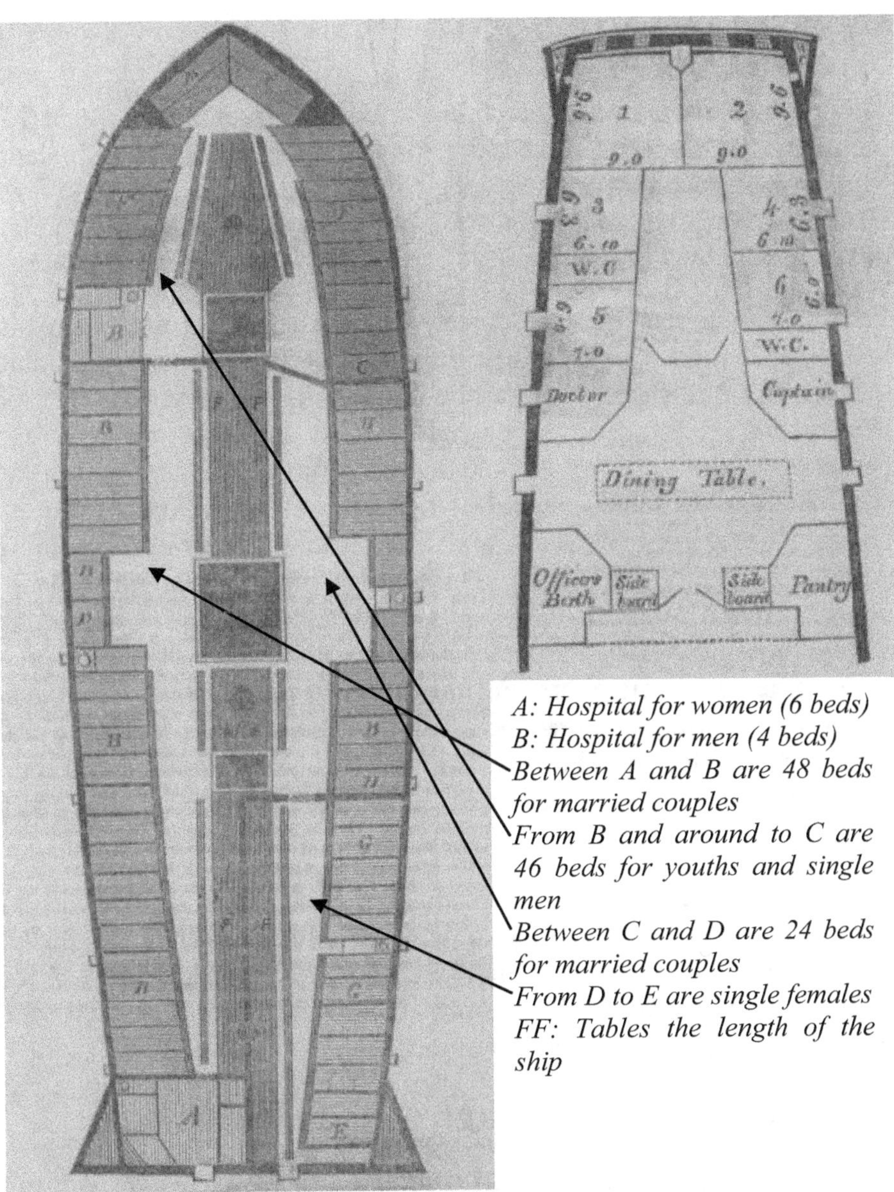

Plan of Emigrant Ship Between Decks (left) and Plan of Cabin Accommodation (right) (courtesy London Illustrated News). The Gananoque may have been slightly different to this plan.

Crew of a Clipper Ship

The average crew of a clipper ship without migrants was about 17, including the Captain, First Mate (or Chief Officer), Second Mate, Midshipman (Apprentice Officer), Ship's Carpenter, Boatswain, 9-10 ordinary seamen and the Cabin Boy who was used for mundane duties and a Cook.

The crew numbers became closer to 40 when emigrants were on board, with additional crew being the Ship's Surgeon and Constable to keep the passenger welfare attended to. There were usually two Cooks; the Passenger's Cook who made food for the steerage passengers and the Ship's Cook for the cabin passengers and crew, who catered for their more refined tastes. A Schoolmaster was on board, to teach the children and a Matron to separate the single woman from the single men. Sometimes there was a Minister on board. Alfred William Craymer's diary for the 1863 *Gananoque* voyage mentions the Carpenter, Boatswain, Stewards, Cook and many other crew members and their high jinks during the voyage, including drinking sessions and stealing. There were usually several Stewards who looked after the Cabin Passengers. Some people took up a job on board to get free passage out.[21] The Matron was often a woman who took on the job in exchange for free passage.

Wages for the crew were on average £7 per month on the way to New Zealand, with good food and comfortable accommodation, but up to a £100 total wage for the home journey, to ensure crew stuck with the ship and didn't desert once in New Zealand. Even with the better wage, desertions were common.[21]

The First Known Voyage of the *Gananoque*

The first journey that has been found for the *Gananoque* is from Liverpool departing 20 August 1858[22] to Hobson's Bay, Melbourne, arriving 25 November 1858, under the command of Archibald Morris with a load of goods for agent Cleve Brothers and Co. There were no passengers on board.[23] It sailed for Mauritius on 31 January 1859 delivering mail there from Australia[24] and probably picking up other cargo, before returning to Great Britain. The next long journey for the ship was the first journey to New Zealand in 1860.

Voyages after 1864

The *Gananoque* was advertised as a "regular trader" with Shaw, Savill & Co. until about June 1870.[25]   However there were no journeys to New Zealand after the last one recorded in the newspapers to New Zealand; 1864 to the Port of Bluff Harbour.

SHAW, SAVILLE and CO'S PASSEN-
GERS' LINE of PACKETS between LONDON
and NEW ZEALAND.—The following first-class
clipper Ships will be continued as REGULAR
TRADERS:—

Ships.	Commanders.	Tons.
Motoaka	W. Stevens	3,000
Chili	T. Turnbull	2,000
Black Swan	G. King	2,000
African	J. Gibson	2,000
Ida Ziegler	W. Reynolds	2,000
Matilda Wattenbach	J. Gondie	2,000
Kensington	W. King	2,000
Avalanche	J. Stott	1,500
Wild Duck	W. C. Bishop	1,500
Gananoque	W. T. Nixon	1,500
Cashmere	C. G. Petherbridge	1,200
Asterope	W. Mitchell	1,200
Evening Star	H. W. Norris	1,200
Dona Anita	J. Smith	1,000
Kinnaird	J. Sinclair	1,000
Geelong	W. Wallace	1,000
Harwood	W. Forsayth	1,000

The ships of this line are all A1 at Lloyd's, and are specially selected for their superior passenger accommodation, and fast-sailing qualities. They are commanded by gentlemen of experience, duly qualified surgeons are carried, and no pains are spared to promote the health and comfort of passengers.

The undersigned, agents for the above fine fleet of ships, are authorized to arrange with settlers here, who may be desirous of bringing their friends in Great Britain to this colony, and who are prepared either to pay the passage money at once, or to give security for payment on arrival of the vessel.

Full particulars may be obtained by applying to

626   NATH. EDWARDS AND CO.

Colonist, 7 December 1866

It appears the *Gananoque* had done so many journeys around the world that it was getting quite worn out. By the early 1870s it disappeared from Lloyd's Register. It then reappeared in 1874 re-rigged as a barque and probably well repaired and ready for a new life as a cargo ship, doing many journeys between the United Kingdom and Canada. The barque had the same tonnage of 785 tons and, was built in Quebec in 1857, the same as the clipper ship *Gananoque*, so it is pretty certain the ships were one and the same.

The Demise of the *Gananoque*

The last few years of the *Gananoque* are interesting as it hit an iceberg – twice! The first collision was on 11 July 1874 as reported in the *Newcastle Courant* of 24 July 1874. The owner at the time was Mr William Johnson of Newcastle. The *Gananoque* left the Tyne in February 1873, bound for Rio de Janeiro.   The barque was then travelling from Quebec back home to Greenock near Glasgow and hit an iceberg off Cape Race, Canada. [26] The barque was picked up and taken to St. John's derelict.   Out of the crew of 17 men, 16 were believed to have been saved, landing at Glace Bay, Nova Scotia, Canada, with one man tragically perishing. The *Dundee Courier and Argus* dated 25 July 1874 listed the local men who were on board including, James Clark (carpenter), David Bell (cook), James Frazer and John Haxton, who came from Dundee and Izat Jones of Scotland. The Captain was from North Shields. The rest of the crew were foreigners.

The *Gananoque* was repaired at St John's, Canada and lasted quite a few more years.   It was sold in 1876, with the following advertisement being placed in the *Liverpool Mercury*, 23 November 1876.

TO CLOSE AN ACCOUNT.
This Day (Thursday), the 23rd instant, at One o'clock, at the Brokers' Saleroom, Walmer-buildings, Water-street (if not previously disposed of by private treaty),
The Barque GANANOQUE,
785 tons register. Built at Quebec under special survey in 1857, and classed seven years A 1 at Lloyd's; sheathed with yellow metal in 1874; is well found in stores, carries a good cargo, and requires very little ballast. Dimensions: Length, 158.2 feet; breadth, 32.8 feet; depth, 21.1 feet.—For further particulars apply to
O. W. KELLOCK & CO., Brokers,
Walmer-buildings, Water-street ; and at
72, Cornhill. London. E.C.

The ship was still employed in cargo runs between Great Britain and Canada until it hit a second iceberg on 10 May 1881, four miles off Bird Rocks, Magdalen Islands, in the Gulf of St Lawrence, not far from the last misfortune. The ship encountered thick fog and the crew couldn't see where they were going. They hit an iceberg which stove in the starboard bow and caused the barque to fill rapidly and sink. The crew managed to get to the safety of Bird Rocks where they sat for two days before they were picked up on 12 May 1881.[26] The sinking meant the end for the *Gananoque* and it became just another shipwreck on the bottom of the ocean.

Tall ship foundering in Arctic Waters, Franklin Expedition – by Walter William May, 1866

Voyage to Lyttelton, New Zealand

(9 February 1860 – 9 May 1860)

Voyage to Lyttelton, New Zealand 1860

The *Gananoque* was advertised in The Times (London) on 17 December 1859.

NEW ZEALAND.—WILLIS and Co.'s CLIPPER PASSENGER PACKETS. The following ships, some of the finest and fastest clippers ever despatched to New Zealand, and fitted up with every comfort and convenience for all classes of passengers, will be despatched as follows:—

Packets.	Burden	Destination.	Date.	Docks.
Constantine ..	1,000	{ Wellington and Nelson }	Jan. 5	St. Katharine's
Avon	1,100	Auckland	Jan. 10	St. Katharine's
Gananoque ..	1,400	Canterbury	Jan. 25	East India
Caduceus	1,600	Auckland	Feb.	East India
Egmont	1,200	Canterbury	Feb.	St. Katharine's

All the above vessels are now in dock, loading and open to inspection. For terms of passage, rates of freight, free grants of land in Auckland, assisted passages to Canterbury, &c., apply to A. Willis, Gann, and Co., New Zealand Emigration Offices, Crosby-square, Bishopsgate. Just published, and sent for six stamps, the New Zealand Handbook, giving a full description of the whole country, and all information needed by the capitalist emigrant and the working man.

NEW ZEALAND.—Willis and Co.'s Line of Passenger Packets.—To follow the Clontarf, and sail punctually on the 25th January.—For CANTERBURY direct, the beautiful clipper packet GANANOQUE, A 1, 785 tons register, 1,200 tons burden, A. MORRIS, Commander; loading in the East India Docks. This fine ship will be despatched with the punctuality which distinguishes these packets. Her saloon is handsome and commodious, with light and roomy cabins, and has very lofty and thoroughly ventilated 'tween decks, offering accommodation for all classes of passengers unsurpassed by any vessel in the trade. For passage, freight, &c., apply to A. Willis, Gann, and Co., No. 3, Crosby-square, Bishopsgate, London, E.C.

The first journey to New Zealand passed quite uneventfully and had a very quick passage of 90 days. A couple of events happened before the passengers boarded however.

The Campbell family had a very bad experience on the journey to board the *Gananoque,* as their daughter Hannah died on the passage from Belfast to Plymouth. It is not mentioned how she died.[27]

The Peagram family had their own share of troubles. Charles Peagram, labourer, aged 35, was crossed out on the passenger list and the name John was added instead. Apparently Charles was arrested for debt before the ship left the docks and Charles's brother John had to take over the care of Charles's children, to take them to

New Zealand.[27] Charles Peagram arrived the following year on 27 July 1861 aboard the *Chrysolite*, listed as a 36 year old labourer.[28] He obviously found a way to come to New Zealand in the end, maybe paying off his debt with hard work. His children would have been so pleased to see him again!

The ship left Gravesend, England on 9 February 1860 with 215 passengers and cargo.   There were 20 in the Chief Cabin, 9 in second cabin, 22 in paid steerage and 166 government assisted immigrants. They left the Downs (an area of sea in the southern North Sea) on 14 February 1860 and it took two days to clear the English Channel where they experienced some very cold weather.

They sighted the peak of San Antonio (likely Santo Antão, Cape Verde) on 26 February. The North East Trades were met with early in the journey and took them down to 3° N by 2 March 1860. This was very quick indeed, being only 17 days from their departure. They saw and spoke many ships at this time including the *Cornigha* from Calcutta for London, 69 days out. This ship wouldn't take letters back to England and the passengers were extremely disappointed. They crossed the Equator on Thursday 8 March 1860 in longitude 23.39° W, which was very quick, taking only 21 days. After this, the boat met with fresh breezes that carried it to the most extreme westerly longitude for the whole journey, 31.28° which would have brought them close to Brazil.

The remote island of Tristan da Cunha. The ship would have had this view as it passed by. Queen Mary's Peak is visible at a height of 2,062 metres. Image taken by Brian Gratwicke

They sighted the Island of Trinidada (probably Trinidad) on 17 March and over the next three days they passed three foreign vessels from France, Norway and America (a "Yankee" vessel). The next Island to be sighted was Tristan da Cunha on 29 March 1860; it has a huge volcanic cone called Saint Mary's Peak reaching 2,062 metres above sea level. This island is the most remote inhabited archipelago in the world and covers 98 square kilometres.[29]

A few days later on 7 April they reached the longitude of the Cape of Good Hope. The journey was very fast from the Cape to New Zealand with a distance of 266 miles covered on one day and the other days not too dissimilar. Prince Edward Islands were sighted on 10 April 1860. The *Gananoque* also struck the correct winds while sailing up the coast of New Zealand, the only hindrance being a 36 hour delay in approaching the Port of Lyttelton due to southerly winds.

On the cargo of the *Gananoque* were some skylarks, a present from the aviaries of a Mr Edward Wilson. The birds were not successfully introduced to New Zealand this time around, much to the annoyance of the Acclimatisation Society. Whether they died on the voyage was not mentioned in the newspapers.[30]

The *Lyttelton Times* on 12 May 1860 described what happened on board, including many fun onboard activities:

"The voyage is described by the passengers as having been most pleasant in all respects, and they give credit to Captain Morris, with his officers, and to Dr. Brown, the Surgeon Superintendent, as having been the promoting causes in this respect. Amusements of all kinds flourished on board among which—to prove the universality of the defence movement—the formation of a Rifle Corps and the drilling of the same was prominent, so long as the fine weather lasted and the ship was tranquil enough to permit the goose-step to be practised. The full and true-particulars of the voyage are written in the *Gananoque Gazette*, a carefully edited board-ship journal, a file of which we have been permitted to peruse. The names and number of the passengers by the *Gananoque*, who are perhaps the best lot ever brought in, will be found below. The health on board throughout the whole voyage was generally excellent; except that a few cases of measles appeared before crossing the line, and disappeared again before the cold weather was reached. The two deaths which occurred were from causes as far as possible removed from epidemic."[31]

Sarah Winfield Brown was employed as a Matron onboard the *Gananoque,* ensuring free passage for her out to her future husband who had already been in New Zealand for three years. She was an unusual candidate for the job, being only 27 years old. Most Matrons were over the age of 40, as this was considered a suitable age.[32] The fact she had a man waiting for her in New Zealand meant that she would hopefully not get distracted by the good looking men on board. Sarah basically had to keep the single men and women apart to avoid any immoral behaviour whilst sailing to the new land. Passengers often became bored on such long journeys so her job would have been a tough one.

The *Gananoque Gazette* is likely not in existence anymore, or maybe it is hidden in someone's cupboard when it should be in a museum. What tales it might tell!

Arrival of the *Gananoque* 1860

The *Gananoque* arrived at Lyttelton on 9 May 1860 after exactly three months, or to be more exact 90 days. [33]

The *Gananoque* was named as "one of the finest ships of her size which we have ever seen in our harbour" in the *Lyttelton Times* on 12 May 1860[31]

In the *Press* dated 27 July 1892 was an article entitled "Racing Men I Have Known" written by a passenger on the *Gananoque* in 1860. The writer went by the pseudonym "Hermit." At the beginning of the article the writer gives an insight into the arrival of the ship at Lyttelton and how people on shore were willing them to be the ship *Burmah* which had not arrived on time.

"It was early in May, 1860, that the good ship *Gananoque* arrived at the Heads of Port Lyttelton, after a remarkably smart passage from England. The present writer was a passenger by her, and was one of the first to welcome the pilot as he came up the side. After the usual greeting between the captain and pilot had taken place, the latter enquired if we had spoken any vessels on the voyage out, and remarked, "When you were first signalled we were all in hopes that the vessel was the *Burmah*, as she is now long overdue." From that day to this nothing has ever been heard of the ill-fated barque, though there was a report that one of her boats had been picked up off the Western coast of Australia.

The *Burmah* and her freight had peculiar interest to horse lovers, as on board, were no less than eleven young thoroughbred stock destined for the stud of Mr W. H. Harris, who was then in partnership with the late Mr D. Innes. Most, if not all of these youngsters had been purchased at Mr Blenkiron's Middle Park sale of 1859, and they were by far the largest and most important shipment to Canterbury that had ever been despatched up to that date." [34]

Samuel Butler in 1858. Creative Commons Attribution 3.0

The novelist Samuel Butler was booked to travel on the *Burmah* but changed to the *Roman Emperor* at the last minute. This decision saved his life.[35]

One of the hazards of sea travel was the ship sinking in the remote open ocean. Ships could encounter a terrible storm or accidentally hit rocks near an island causing the boat to sink quickly. Lifeboats could be launched but the chances of being found were sometimes very slim and most of the time all souls on board would be lost.

Lyttelton Harbour in 1863, a panoramic view from the Bridle Path. Courtesy London Illustrated News.

FIRST SHIP FOR CALLAO.

THE fine clipper ship GANANOQUE will sail for the above port about the 15th JUNE.

Passengers returning home should avail themselves of this opportunity.

For further particulars, apply to the CAPTAIN on board, or

DALGETY, BUCKLEY & CO.,

Agents.

Lyttelton Times, 2 June 1860

Gananoque Cargo 1860

In the Gananoque, Dalgety & Co., agents; 5 hhds. wine, 16 qr. casks do, 8 octave do, 226 tons coals, 2 cases, Order; 1 case apparel, Docker; 3 cases saddlery, 2 casks do, Earle; 1 cart, Wishart; 1 case watches, Travis; 7 casks, 14 boxes, Nosworthy; 1 case hardware, 2 pkgs. leather, 1 case reel cotton, Burnell & Bennett; 1 case, Kay; 1 box apparel, Voisin; 1 case, Raxworthy; 1 cask, Neeve; 1 case saddlery, T. Fisher; 1 crate chairs, Hawley; 1 case apparel, Hubbard; 1 case do, Minchener; 6 casks seeds, McDonald & Dodds; 1 case, T. C. Smith; 1 box apparel, Greaves; 1 case, Mountfort; 1 case apparel, J. C. Watts Russell; 3 casks, Gresson; 40 cart arms, 1 cask bolts, 6 hhds. beer, 1 case, Cookson and Co.; 1 case brushware, 3 bales mats, 39 cases, Heywood; 1 pkg. books, Dawe; 1 box apparel, King; 1 cask apple pips, Horrell; 1 puncheon seeds, 5 casks, do, 1 box do, Hislop; 1 box apparel, Jeffreys; 1 crate earthenware, Brown, Cox & Co.; 8 qr. casks wine, Strouts; 2 cases, Leake; 1 case apparel, Dalziel; 1 case do, Turnbull & Hilson; 1 box, Webb; 1 piano, 1 case, the Bishop of Christchurch; 1 box apparel, Turner; 1 box fruit trees, Whitcombe; 1 box apparel, Anson; 1 box books, Bell; 3 cases books, his Honor the Superintendent; 1 case apparel, Wormald; 1 box do, Raven; 1 case, Younger; 1 box tools, White; 3 cases, Mellish; 1 box, Poigndestre; 27 casks seeds, 15 casks spirits, 12 cases cordials, R. Waitt; 31 casks seeds, Walker; 10 barrels rum, 5 qr. casks whiskey, 10 do. sherry, 4 octaves do, 8 qr. casks port, 3 octaves do, 70 cases port and sherry, 20 hhds. 20 brls. ale, 32 casks soda, 63 cases oilmen's stores, 1 case apparel, 7 cases confectionery, 1 cask, 100 casks bottled beer, 2 packages, dog cart, &c., 135 water casks, 23 tons coals, 1 cooking apparatus, 5 cases, Dalgety & Co.; 2 hhds. seeds, Toswill; 2 boxes, Pollard; 7 trunks boots, Goodman; 4 casks seeds, Clark; 1 hhd. rum, 1 do gin, Wilson; 1 case apparel, Gould & Miles; 2 boxes, Low; 1 piano, Sutcliffe; 1 box, Torlesse; 1 case apparel, D'Auvergne; 1 box, Stevens; 1 case, Papperill; 1 package apparel, Ross; 1 box, Sladden; 1 case apparel, 2 casks cider, Kennaway; 1 case books, Bradwell; 1 box apparel, Mannering, 1 case, Harman; 2 packages, Ford; 1 case furniture, Smith; 1 case apparel, Sadler; 14 casks, 10 cases, 1 box, Reece; 6 cases confectionery, 1 tierce earthenware, 6 chests tea, 3 cases coffee, 6 do raisins, 5 do currants, 2 do chicory, 1 do figs, 5 cases, Latter; 17 cases, 5 bales, 3 trunks, G. Gould; 7 crates, 28 cases, 1 tierce, 1 bundle lead pipe, 1 cask shot, 3 bundles spades, 6 casks nails, 1 box, 9 casks, 2 baskets, 2 bundles, 2 machines, 3 trunks, 4 bales, 5 iron pipes, 4 packages, Barrett, Brothers; 1 case apparel, Beard; 1 package agricultural implements, Matthew; 6 cases, 2 barrels, 1 hhd., 12 kegs, 5000 bricks, F. N. Campbell & Co.; 2 cases books, Ferguson; 3 packages, dog cart; 8 cases, Knyvett; 2 crates, 6 cases, Ashton; 1 case, Garland.

List of cargo on the Gananoque, Lyttelton Times, 12 May 1860

Births and Deaths on the *Gananoque*

Births on Board

Green, Morris Gananoque — son of Susan and Samuel Green on 18 February 1860.

Scully — son of W.C. Scully on 23 April 1860.

Deaths on board

Stevenson, Sarah — wife of Mr J. Stevenson, aged 38 on 3 March 1860.

Ryan, Robert — son of Mr Thomas Ryan, aged 1 yr 9mths on 5 April 1860.

Morris Gananoque Green was named after Captain Archibald Morris and the name of the ship he was born on. He lived to the grand old age of 83 years old, dying in 1943 in New Zealand.

Summary of Trades on Board

The passenger list summarised the trades on board the ship, making interesting reading. The most common trade on board was Farm Labourer.

Land – Farm Labourers 32, General Labourers 5, Gardeners 4, Ploughmen, 5; Miner, 1.
Stock – Shepherd, 1.
Iron – Blacksmith, 1.
Wood – Cabinet Maker, 1; Joiner, 1; Carpenters, 2.
Leather – Saddler, 1.
Miscellaneous – Domestic Servant, 1; Miller, 1; Oilman, 1; Slater, 1; Schoolmaster, 1.
Single Women – Domestic Servants, 15; Cook, 1; Dairywomen, 3; Factory Girl, 1; Needlewomen, 3; Nursery Governess, 1.

A Captain's Engagement

The journey on the *Gananoque* in 1860 was clearly an enjoyable one given the accounts in newspapers. It appears that Captain Archibald Morris had plenty of leisure time while on board, as he was romancing one of his passengers and became engaged to her before arrival in New Zealand. Captain Morris and the mystery passenger were married while the ship was sitting in Lyttelton Harbour. A "pleasant evening" was spent on board celebrating the wedding and the evening wound up with a speech from the Chief Officer. He proposed a toast to the Captain and his bride's health and the people on board sang "They are jolly good fellows." Several *Gananoque* passengers then left the boat and boarded the brig *Fanny A. Garrigues* to travel on to Otago.[36] Captain Morris took the ship back to the United Kingdom on 21 July 1860 via Callao, Peru where ships picked up loads of guano. He had exports onboard from New Zealand including some rum. [37] Presumably his new wife was at his side on the journey back; her plan to settle in New Zealand being slightly disrupted!

The Guano Trade

It appears that the *Gananoque* was involved in the guano trade, like many ships in those days. It made the long journey back to the United Kingdom more economic for the owners.

An interesting article in the North Otago Times, 10 January 1871[38] talks about the guano trade in the 19th century and what the port of Callao was like. A sailing ship took about six weeks to do the journey from Dunedin to Callao. The article says "All vessels are obliged to clear here [Callao] on their arrival and departure. The streets have been widened, the houses improved, and altogether the town looks well from the bay, though it does not bear a close inspection so well, having all the abominations of South American ports."

Numerous vessels crowded the bay. "The harbor generally presents a very lively scene in the number of large and small craft, snuff-colored guano ships, coal ships, steamers, men-of-war, and hundreds of row boats, with white duck awnings, glancing along the placid waters, conveying passengers to and from the shipping."

On one of the Chinchas Islands it was estimated in 1850 that there was a depth of 100 feet of guano on the centre of the island gradually decreasing towards the edges, resting on granite underneath. Its main use was for fertiliser for agriculture.[38]

The Harbour at Callao, c.1866 (Mánuel A Fuentes)

One can just imagine the lively scene presented to Archibald Morris's new wife, with new adventures she could never have dreamed of. What became of the new couple after their trip back to Great Britain we can only guess at. Archibald didn't make a trip back on the *Gananoque* to New Zealand again, the next commander being Captain Nixon.

WANTED,—By a Young ENGLISH-WOMAN, arrived by the Gananoque, a situation as HOUSEMAID or PLAIN COOK, in a gentleman's family.

Apply to A.N., at the Union Printing Office, Christchurch.

Gananoque advertisement, Lyttelton Times, 27 June 1860

THE GANANOQUE

The saloon passengers by this ship, before their arrival, presented Captain Morris with a purse containing a sum of money to be expended in the purchase of a piece of plate, as a memento of their pleasant voyage. The presentation of the memorial was accompanied by the following address:—

"To A. Morris, Esquire.

"We, the undersigned passengers of the Gananoque have the greatest pleasure in offering you the accompanying purse, to be expended in the purchase of some small but enduring testimonial of the sincere esteem and respect with which we regard you.

"We are fully convinced that it has seldom been the lot of any passengers to sail with a Captain, who has made himself so universally and so justly popular, as well by attention to the comfort of all, as by zeal often displayed in aiding attempts to lighten the monotony more or less attendant on every long voyage.

"Those of us who have been travellers before are perhaps in a better position to appreciate the general uprightness and impartiality of your conduct, and the urbanity with which you have always treated us.

"As a commander and navigator, we have ever had every confidence in you, a confidence which has certainly not been lessened by the very quick passage to New Zealand which we have just made; while as a man we shall always remember you as a friend whom we would be only too glad to meet again, and to whom we wish every good thing that could possibly be desired.

The fore-cabin passengers have presented Captain Morris, with the following address on their own behalf:—

"To A. Morris, Esq., Commander of the Ship Gananoque.

'Sir,—We, who have been fore-cabin passengers in the Gananoque, during the prosperous passage just completed, wish to express the high esteem in which you are held by one and all of us, and our admiration of your character, both as commander of a ship, and as an amiable and just man. The harmony which has existed during the passage, the confidence with which you have inspired us, and the uniform kindness with which we have been treated, while speaking so highly of your qualifications as a commander, have induced us to offer this, the only tribute in our power to offer merit.

In your attempts to lighten and alleviate our trials during the voyage, you have been ably seconded by your officers, to whom, as well as yourself, we wish every success in life, and do assure you you will ever be remembered with gratitude and affection.

May, 1860.

Dr. Brown has been complimented by the Emigrants on board as follows :—

" To John Ansell Brown, Esq., Surgeon of the Ship Gananoque.

" Sir,—We the undersigned are deeply impressed with thankfulness that we have been so fortunate as to sail with such an officer as yourself, placed in the position which you occupy towards us. We are satisfied that none could have more efficiently discharged the duties of your office, irksome as they sometimes were, and we know that none could have performed those duties with greater courtesy and politeness, or with kinder regard to our feelings, or more untiring desire to promote our comfort and health.

" The medical officer of a ship is either the chief friend or the bugbear of the emigrant ; and we congratulate and compliment you on the graceful manner in which you have secured our warmest thanks for past kindness; with sincerest wishes for your future prosperity and happiness.

Lyttelton Times, 16 May 1860

Map of the Journey of the *Gananoque*

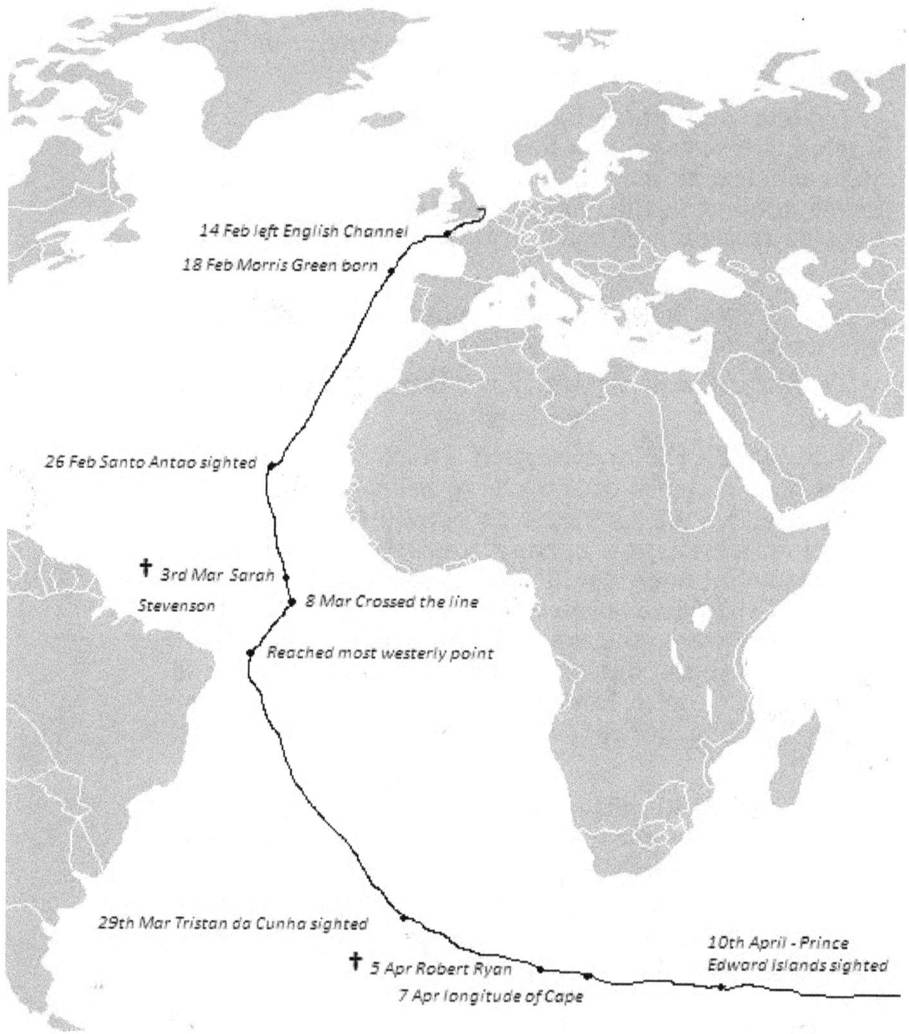

(9 February 1860 – 9 May 1860)

Archibald Morris Vs Thomas Bailey

In May 1858, Thomas Bailey was sole owner of the *Gananoque* and offered Archibald Morris a 1/8th share in the ship, also becoming master. He received £15 per month and a third of the gross cabin passage money and a half of the cabin freight. Before he made a cargo journey to Melbourne, Australia, he received the following letter from Thomas Bailey:

"Liverpool, 9th Aug. 1858

"Dear Sir, - The Gananoque being about to proceed on a voyage to Melbourne, and perhaps other places, I offer you the command of that ship on the following terms: Your pay being 15l. per month, to commence the 1st of this month. The cabin passage-money – the profits, if any, to be equally divided; any light freight you may bring home in the poop, all other parts of the ship being full, you will have one-third freight. All necessary travelling expenses, when on ship's duty, will be paid you. You will use the utmost economy and despatch, &c., &c. T. Bailey"

Archibald accepted these terms. The ship arrived back in London on 8 December 1859 and in the meantime Thomas Bailey had signed up with Willis, Gann & Co. for a trip to New Zealand carrying passengers. Archibald presumed that without a new contract his old contract still stood and he would receive the same terms. Thomas Bailey had told Archibald that he would receive an additional gratuity of forty or forty-five guineas from Willis, Gann & Co. for the journey. After arriving back in England in March 1861, Archibald quit his job on the ship, and when he was sorting out his payment, Thomas refused to pay Archibald his share of the cabin passenger profits. He had been paid 42l. by Willis, Gann & Co. which was in line with the usual Australian ship master rates.

The judgement on this case was that Archibald deserved a share in the cabin passage-money profits as there was no agreement to say otherwise and also that the previous agreement still stood.

So Archibald Morris made a tidy extra profit from this journey and could move on with his life as a newly wed man!

Passengers on the Lyttelton Voyage 1860

Passengers on the Lyttelton Voyage 1860

Amor

Richard Mullins Amor was born in 1837 in Bruton, Somerset, England. Richard married Elizabeth Wilton in early 1860, just before immigrating to New Zealand onboard the *Gananoque* which departed on 9 February 1860. They had at least seven children; four girls and three boys. The oldest, Elizabeth, was born in Doyleston, Canterbury, New Zealand in 1862[39] Richard died in 1885 aged only 48 and Elizabeth in 1915 aged 79 in Doyleston, Canterbury. Richard and Elizabeth are buried in Ellesmere Cemetery.

Ayers

Aaron Ayers was born in Gloucester, England in 1836. He married Isabella Eliza Williams in 1859, daughter of Mr. F. F. Williams of London. They travelled to Lyttelton on the *Gananoque* in 1860. Aaron became a hairdresser and tobacconist in Christchurch. In 1880 he changed his profession to auctioneer and then became the senior partner at a firm called Ayers, Beauchamp and Co. which was situated in Cashel Street. He became a member of the Linwood Borough Council and eventually became Mayor of the City of Christchurch. Aaron died on 15 September 1900 and at the time of his death had four sons and four daughters living.[40]

Mr Aaron Ayers

Brann

John Henry Charles Brann was born in Warehorne, Kent in 1827. He was a teacher for a short time in England before travelling to New Zealand. He was schoolmaster on the voyage out to New Zealand on the *Gananoque*. John moved to Wellington and married Lucy Martha Woodward in 1866. As a teacher, John was an assistant to a Mr. E. Toomath and then he ran his own private school for fifteen years in Boulcott Street, Wellington. He closed the school and then worked for the Education Board for fourteen years mainly in Clareville and Carterton, retiring in 1894. John and Lucy had three daughters and one son living at the time of his biography in the Cyclopedia of New Zealand.[41] They were settlers of No. 2 Line, Wanganui. Lucy died in 1902 after a short illness in Wanganui.[42]

Breakwell

John Breakwell was born in 1835 in Coreley, Shropshire, England. He married Ellen Parton in 1856 and they sailed to Lyttelton on the *Gananoque* in 1860. They had nine children, six boys and three girls, all born in New Zealand.[43] Alfred Breakwell was the oldest child, born on 1 January 1861 in Christchurch. The family was living in Papanui at the time and John was a millwright.[44] The family then moved to Milford, near Temuka. John went bankrupt in about 1875.[45]

Brown

Sarah Winfield Brown was born in Dorking, Surrey in 1830. She followed her future husband, James Potts, to New Zealand. James arrived on the *Glentanner* in 1857 and Sarah followed in 1860 on the *Gananoque*. They married on 11 June 1860 at St Michael and All Angels, Christchurch. They had four children, but two were stillborn and two died as infants. James Potts died in 1879, leaving Sarah a childless widow. She remarried in 1882 to widower Karl Philipp Meng and gained three stepdaughters. Sarah was a wonderful stepmother to the girls. Karl died in 1885. Sarah owned a lot of property including

*Sarah Winfield
Meng nee Brown*

houses at the corner of Halkett and Antigua Streets, Christchurch which she rented out. Sarah died in 1904 in Antigua Street, Christchurch and was buried in Addington Cemetery.[46]

Crampton

George William Crampton was born in County Wicklow, Ireland in 1843. He travelled to Lyttelton on the *Gananoque* in 1860 and settled near Amberley where he became a shepherd for seven years. He then became a farmer until 1898, settling at Cheviot. He was considered one of the original settlers of the Cheviot area and had a farm called *Green Ridge,* which consisted of 303 acres of leased land. George was Secretary of the Loyal Cheviot Lodge of Oddfellows. George married Margaret Burn in 1869 and they had six sons and three daughters.[47]

Mr. G. W. Crampton

Green

Samuel Green and his wife Susan were passengers on the *Gananoque* in 1860. Susan gave birth to son Morris Gananoque Green while on board the ship. He was named after the Captain and the ship he was born on, and lived into his eighties. Samuel Green died in about 1866, only six years after they arrived, and Susan married again in 1869 to Richard Offwood, a carrier. Susan died in 1904. Her obituary stated that "her husband and a large number of children and grandchildren" survived her.[48]

Humm

William Humm was born in Great Henny, Essex, England in 1837 and was brought up in a farming family. He married Eliza Owens, born 1839 in Essex, and they came to New Zealand on the *Gananoque* in 1860. William's first occupation in Christchurch was digging and bagging potatoes, before working at the Royal Hotel earning £1 per week. In 1864, William bought fifty acres of land at

Mr William Humm

Weedons. He used to burn straw on the fire as wood and coal were too expensive at that time. In 1873 he moved to Waddington and bought 244 acres. It was called *Applecroft Farm*. He worked extremely hard to turn a piece of land with native tussock into a working farm, eventually subdividing and building a homestead and outbuildings. He became financially successful from all his hard work. He was closely associated with the Waddington Primitive Methodist Church. William and his wife Eliza had seven sons and four daughters. In about 1900 they had twenty-seven grandchildren.[49]

Karslake

John Karslake Karslake was born in England. John settled in the Cheviot area in 1861, and in about 1863 bought the Waireka run in the Malvern district in partnership with Thomas Anson. They then bought Run 210 in February 1868 and Run 277 (which was adjacent to Run 210) in about 1870. The two runs were combined to make the Torlesse Station, named after Mount Torlesse. John was either the brother or nephew of John Burgess Karslake, an English lawyer and politician. John K. Karslake won the Coleridge electorate in 1871. He resigned in 1872 to return to England, but drowned on the return voyage on 21 June 1872.[50]

Kidd

Joshua Kidd was born in 1842 in Perthshire, Scotland, where he was brought up in the country. He travelled to Lyttelton on the *Gananoque* in 1860 and spent a year at Maori Bush in North Canterbury. He then settled in Amberley and became a shepherd at Mount Brown Estate for over forty years. Joshua married Mary Johnston in 1873 and together they had six sons and three daughters. Joshua's wife Mary was born in Tasmania in 1849 and travelled to Wellington, New Zealand as an infant, arriving January 1850.[51]

Mr and Mrs J. Kidd

Lovesay

Emma Lovesay, (sometimes spelt Lovesey or Loveday) born about 1838 in Middlesex, England, travelled on the *Gananoque* with two aunts (Emma Newnham and Jane Kitchingham) and several cousins from the Kitchingham family. In the passenger list she was named as a domestic servant. She married Joseph Jackson on 15 April 1862 at the Wesleyan Chapel in Christchurch.[44] They had a family of at least six boys and three girls. Emma died in 1924 aged 86 years old.[52]

Mellars

George Frederick Mellars was born in Worksop, Nottinghamshire, England in 1832. He spent about 15 years working at sea before he arrived on the ship *Gananoque* (spelt Gannonoak in the Cyclopedia of New Zealand). He was third mate at the time and resigned from the position so he could settle in New Zealand. He worked in the timber business in both Woodend and Oxford for several years. George got caught up in the gold rush for about six months in Hokitika and then went to Thames in 1868 chasing the gold. After a short time he moved to Auckland and eventually settled in Ohaupo in 1869.

Mr. and Mrs. G. F. Mellars

He started working in the sawmilling business and in 1888 he bought 1000 acres of land in Taupiri, where he established a sawmill. He stayed in the business until 1899. He then worked in the flax business. A fourteen horse-power steam engine drove the machinery in his flax mill. Flax was purchased through a contract with the local Maori. In 1863, George married Mary Rose Gibbs, daughter of Mr G. Gibbs and they had seven daughters and five sons. George died in 1904 and Mary Rose died in 1908.[53]

Milne

David Milne was born in Scotland in 1859 and travelled with his parents to on the *Gananoque.* He was a baby at the time. His family acquired a sheep run at Mohaka. David lived there for many years and was in partnership with his father and brother. The partnership was dissolved and David moved to Petane and lived at a homestead called *Burnside* which was situated seven miles from Napier. The property was 15 acres in size with another 785 acres being tenanted out. David married Sarah Matilda Bowman in 1893, daughter of George Bowman who was a well known Napier settler. They had two sons and one daughter.[54]

Mr D. Milne

McKenzie

Alexander McKenzie was from Dundee, Scotland, born in 1848 and travelled on the *Gananoque* aged 11 with his family. He joined the locomotive service and in 1906 became a locomotive inspector for the South Island, retiring in 1912. He married Mary Ann Thompson at St Andrew's Church, Christchurch by the Rev. C. Fraser in 1870. In 1930 they celebrated their diamond wedding anniversary. They lived at Lancaster Street, Linwood, Christchurch. They had a family of six, but at the time of their diamond wedding only two were still alive, and they had seven grandchildren and one great grandchild. [55]

Newnham

Emma Newnham was born in London in 1815 and travelled to New Zealand on the *Gananoque* in 1860. She married John Guilford in 1863. John arrived on the *Castle Eden* in 1851 with his first wife Ann, née Plank, who died in 1862 in Christchurch. In 1862, John bought 95 acres at Arowhenua and 10 acres at Raukapaka Bush, Geraldine. Emma died in Christchurch in 1890 and is buried in Addington Cemetery. John then went up to Wanganui to be with his son James. John died in 1895 and was buried in Wanganui.[56]

Peagram

Charles Henry Peagram arrived with his family on the *Gananoque* in 1860, aged 13. His first shearing season was in 1867 at Racecourse Hill, which was owned by Rhodes and Wilkin and managed by Mr Davison, and also on Double Hill, which was owned by a Mr Palmer. Apart from two seasons in the North Island, he did all his shearing in Canterbury and he was exclusively a blade shearer. He could get through 6000 to 7000 sheep in a season. At 80 years old he was still shearing, having done fifty-seven years in the profession. He was shearing sheep at Bankside and managed to do 84 sheep, an amazing feat for an octogenarian. Charles married Eliza Jane Beasley in 1868 and they had at least three children. Charles died in 1936, aged an amazing 89 years old.[57]

In 1907 there was a reunion of pioneers who came on the first four ships and other early ships, and a Mr. E. Peagram attended with his ship listed as *Gananoque*.[58] This was probably Edward Peagram, Charles's brother, who was 11 when he came out to New Zealand.

Pepper

Rachel Pepper nee Haughey was born about 1836 in Ireland. She travelled with her husband Andrew Pepper, and son, William John, on the *Gananoque*. Andrew died on 24 August 1861 after losing his way and drowning in the Avon River.[59] He had been "drinking freely" at the White Hart Hotel and walked home down a by-road near Woodford's Mill. It took until 8 September 1861 for his body to be found after a dog pulled off Andrew's cap and took it to his owner, Mr Hawkes.[60] Rachel remarried to John Goggin on 28 May 1864.[44] Many years later, in 1920, there was a family gathering for the 60th anniversary of her arriving in New Zealand on the *Gananoque*. The diamond jubilee was held at the family house at the corner of Hills Road and Gresford Street, with lots of family present and much music and celebrations. Three generations were present at the evening and "Mrs. Goggin was the recipient of many compliments."[61] Rachel lived to 90 years old, passing away in 1926.[62]

Street

Arthur and Louisa Street were living in Middlesex before they left on the *Gananoque* in 1860. They had at least two children including a daughter, Mary Louisa in 1860, and a son, Frank John in 1864.[62] After arriving, Arthur set up business as a painter and was in the firm Allright and Street, painters. [63] Arthur died of typhoid in 1865, aged 29, in Canterbury Street, Lyttelton.[64]

Stringer

Joseph Henry Stringer was born in 1837 in London. At age 17 he went to fight in the Crimean war and was awarded a medal for going over a parapet under fire. He was also selected by the Emperor Napoleon for one of the 500 French war medals. He also had British and Turkish war medals. He resigned from the army to travel to New Zealand on the *Gananoque*. He explored around Lake Wakatipu, and eventually went back to Canterbury where he married Elizabeth Yeomanson in 1863. When the first train ran on the Canterbury Railway, Joseph was on the staff. Elizabeth and Joseph had six sons and four daughters, and at the time of Joseph's death in 1920 he had 33 grandchildren and three great-grandchildren.[65]

Thompson

William John Thompson was born in County Down, Ireland in 1859 and travelled with his parents, Richard Thompson and Jane, née Pepper,[66] and older brother, Andrew, as an infant on board the *Gananoque*. He was brought up in the country. In New Zealand he started his own farm, called *Marshdale,* in Cust in 1882. He ended up with 475 acres. He mainly undertook sheep farming. William was a member of the Summerhill School committee. He married Jane Eliza Bennett of West Eyreton, in August 1894 and together they had two sons and one daughter.[67]

Mr. and Mrs. W. J. Thompson

Voyage to Auckland, New Zealand
(7 July 1861 – 18 October 1861)

Voyage to Auckland, New Zealand, 1861

Almost immediately after the *Gananoque* returned to London from the first voyage to New Zealand the ship was loading for the second voyage, this time under the flag of Shaw, Savill & Co.

The ship sailed from Gravesend on 7 July 1861[68] and the Downs on 9 July 1861 with Captain William Thomas Nixon commanding and 126 passengers. North of the Equator the ship sighted Palma (La Palma, Canary Islands) and sailed inside the Cape de Verde islands (now Cape Verde). It took just over a month to cross the Equator, which took place on 12 August 1861 at 20° W longitude. The North East Trades were fairly good until about 15° N. Then the ship was detained for about 15 to 16 days when the North East trade wind stopped blowing and the ship was travelling very slowly. Light South East Trades then prevailed and the ship passed 30° S latitude, 31° W longitude. It then passed the meridian of the Cape of Good Hope on 6 September 1861 and "ran down the easting" with steady breezes at the latitude of about 44° S.

On 15 September it was a terrible day when the third officer, Mr. Lovell Jones, was knocked overboard by the main topmast studding-sail sheet. The ship was sailing fast at about 12 knots and the sea was rough. A lifebuoy and ropes were thrown to him, and the lifeboat lowered, but they didn't manage to save his life and he tragically drowned. According to the newspapers, if the *Gananoque* had been fitted with Kynaston's disengaging hooks, like the H.M. ship *Cossack*, the man's life may have been saved.[69] These hooks were invented in 1857 by Captain Augustus Frederick Kynaston to allow ships' lifeboats to be rapidly and safely launched while at sea.[70] The crew must have taken too long to launch the lifeboat on board the *Gananoque* and hence Mr Lovell Jones drowned.

On 24 September there was a howling gale, which blew from North West to South West and lasted for four days. The ship was skimming quickly across the sea for four days with a wild and scary sea around them. The passengers were battened down in the hull for four days.[71] The sea was breaking violently over the port quarter of the ship. This washed away the poop rails on the port side of the ship and smashed inwardly the fore boat and long boat. The stern cabin windows and skylight were smashed and this caused the after cabins to be flooded badly. The windows in the poop awning were also broken. There were fowl coops on board. Chickens were often kept on board to provide fresh eggs to the passengers and also for meat. The fowl coops (which may have contained live chickens, although this isn't mentioned) were washed overboard into the sea and also anything that wasn't tied down was swept away. The passengers would have feared for their lives, locked away inside the ship. People often huddled together praying to God that the storm would end soon and they would all survive. Luckily the *Gananoque* got through the storm.

A young man of 27 died on board on 29 September. His name was James Houston, a steerage passenger, and he suddenly dropped dead on the deck of the ship. A post mortem revealed he had heart disease. He had not told anyone of any illness while on board so his death was a shock to everyone.[72]

The magnificent Cape Pillar, Tasmania.

The passengers and crew must have breathed a sigh of relief as suddenly there was good weather, which started before the South West Cape of Tasmania (Cape Pillar), which they passed on 6

October 1861. The winds became "light and contrary", i.e. were blowing this way and that, for several days until they sighted the North Cape of New Zealand at 3.30pm on the 16 October and Tiri Tiri Matangi Island on 17 October. The ship arrived in the Waitemata harbour, Auckland on 18 October 1861.

Waitemata Harbour 1869 (Sir George Grey Special Collections, Auckland Libraries, 1-W473)

A newspaper article stated that "She brought a considerable number of passengers of a superior class, among them being Mr. David Nathan and family, who were returning to their land of adoption." Mr. David Nathan arrived in New Zealand around 1840 or earlier and was one of the first Englishmen to set up business in the colony.

There was one birth on board but no mention of who gave birth or the name of the baby in the newspapers.[33]

The voyage took 101 days. There is no surviving official passenger list for this journey, only newspaper reports that list 103 passengers.[68]

To the Captain and Officers of the 'Gananoque.'

Auckland, October 19th, 1861.

GENTLEMEN,—We, the undersigned, upon our arrival in Auckland, take this opportunity of expressing our gratitude for the kindness and consideration which we have at all times received at your hands during the period occupied in our passage from London to New Zealand; and beg your acceptance of this address as a slight acknowledgment of your attention to our comfort, together with our sincere wishes for your welfare and that of your families.

We remain, Gentlemen,

Yours very truly.

D. Nathan
T. Lloyd, J. P.
W. F. Lodge
M. Boyd
A. Lodge
R. Nathan
S. Nathan
A. Coote
L. Nathan
W. T. Lloyd, Capt. R.E.
W. G. Stack
C. T. Lloyd
C. M. North
L. A. Hart
G. S. Horner
L. A. Nathan
L. Nathan
A. Wintle
F. G. Eaton
J. B. Hamilton
A. Wells
J. Potts
W. Butcher
P. McAlester, junr.

G. Rome
J. L. Clark
P. McAlester, senr., & family
R. McGruthan
C. G. Hustwick
R. Bruce
Mrs. R. Bruce
J. G. Bruce
R. A. Young
B. McAlester
H. McAlester
J. Buchanan
M. Buchanan
W. McAlester
A. Smellie
N. Divine
W. Divine
J. Ryan
M. Fitzgerald
W. Leslie
A. Steven
A. Ferguson
W. Bryce
E. Buchanan, wife & family

A. Buchanan
E. Buchanan
C. Sinclair
J. H. Buchanan
P. Moylan
M. Moylan
G. D. Chamberlain
J. Ryan
D. Galbraith
J. Hay
J. Fenton & wife
J. Edmiston, wife & children
R. Stokes
D. Newman and wife
W. B. Walton
T. Wates
A. Tait
R. McNeil
I. Harwood
R. Thomson
C. Hall
J. Stichbury

Daily Southern Cross, 29 October 1861

To W. T. Nixon, Commander of the Ship 'Gananoque.'

DEAR SIR,—In the name of the undermentioned passengers, we beg your acceptance of this small token of our regard, for the great kindness and attention we have always received at your hands.

Presented by the Passengers to W. T. Nixon, Esq., Commander of the 'Gananoque,' for his uniform kindness and attention.

October 25th, 1861.

Mr. D. Nathan	W. C. Lloyd	Mr. C. M. North
Mrs. Nathan and family	Miss A. Coote	Mr. B. Bruce
	Mr. W. G. Stack	Mr. P. McAlister
Mr. L. Nathan	Mr. L. Hart	Mr. J. Potte
Mr. F. Lloyd	Mr. G. S. Horner	Mr. F. Eaton
Mrs. Lloyd	M. W. Lodge	Mr. R. Thompson
Capt. Lloyd	Mrs. Lodge	

LADIES AND GENTLEMEN,—I beg to acknowledge with very lively gratification the receipt of your kind address to me and the officers of the Ship 'Gananoque,' upon this, the termination of our voyage from England, also of the handsome Testimonial which you have presented to myself.

The warm expressions of satisfaction with which you have been pleased to intimate success in the endeavors made to render the voyage agreeable, will be ever remembered in conjunction with the kindly disposition so uniformly manifested by you throughout the voyage, without which success would have been impracticable on the part of myself and officers of the ship.

With our sincere thanks and every kind wish for your future welfare and enjoyment in this fine country.

I am, ladies and gentlemen,
Most truly and faithfully yours,
W. THOMAS NIXON.

Daily Southern Cross, 29 October 1861

IS now entered at the Customs, and ready for discharge alongside the Queen-street Wharf. It is therefore required that all entries of shipments be passed without delay, otherwise goods to hand not cleared will be landed and stored at the Queen's Warehouse at expense and risk of consignees.

D. NATHAN & CO.,

Agents.

For London Direct.

THE New A1 Clipper Ship 'GANANOQUE,' 785 tons register, W. T. Nixon, Commander, will be ready to receive Wool and other produce for homeward cargo—a large portion of which is now under engagement—about the first of November.

Passengers for England are requested to inspect the spacious accommodation offered by this ship, of latest improvement.

For freight and passage apply to

D. NATHAN & CO.

Agents.

Daily Southern Cross, 22 October 1861

CRICKET! CRICKET!! CRICKET!!

EX 'GANANOQUE.'

A LARGE assortment of Clapshaw's and Sons, celebrated Cricket BATS, BALLS AND STUMPS.

OWEN & FENDELOW,

Ironmongers and Importers,

Upper Queen-street,

Auckland.

Daily Southern Cross, 19 November 1861

Map of the Journey of the *Gananoque* 1861

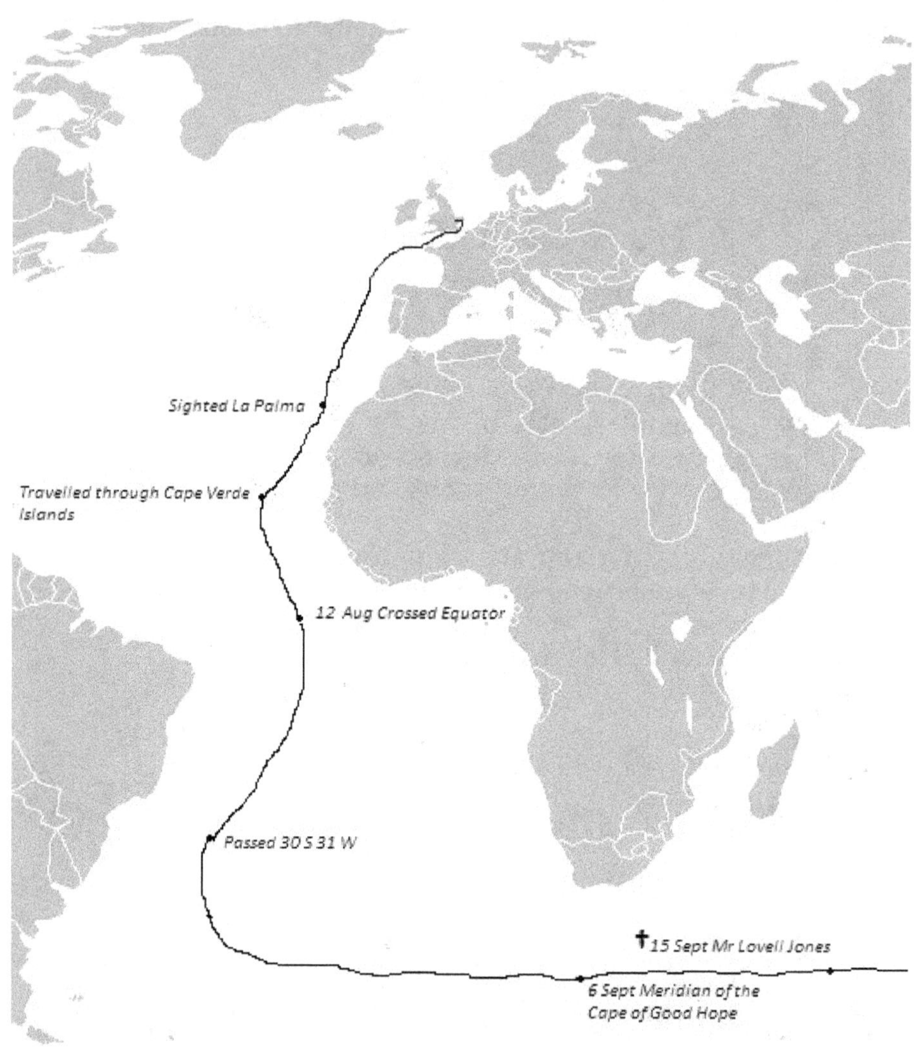

(7 July 1861 – 18 October 1861)

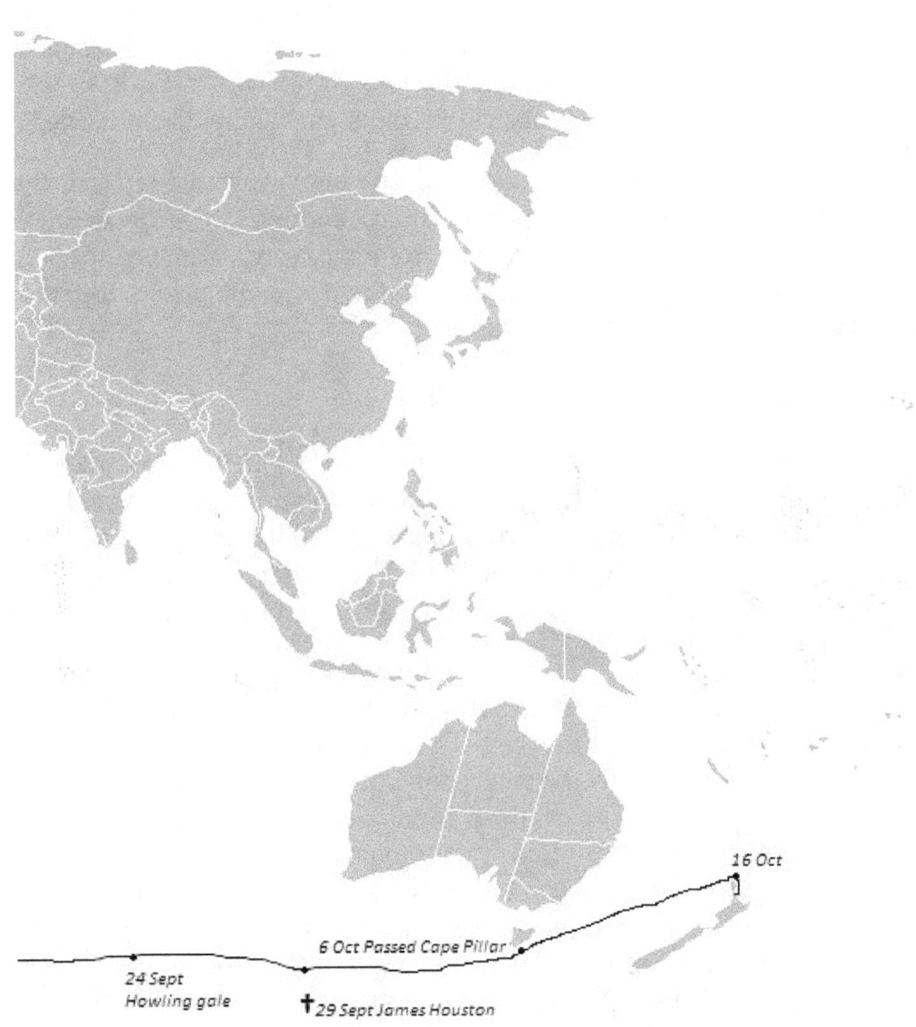

Gananoque Cargo 1861

The newspapers said, "The stocks of drapery and soft goods generally are large. There were considerable additions made by the *Gananoque* from London, and the *Kate* from Sydney, to the stocks previously in the merchants' hands; and these will be still further increased by the consignments to arrive per early ships from home."

"During the past month we have had one arrival from England, the *Gananoque*, with a cargo of general merchandize; one from Sydney, the *Kate*, with a similar cargo one from the South Sea Islands, the *Osprey*, with tropical produce, which fetched high prices together with a large fleet of coasting vessels." [73]

Charges of Importing Arms

In the *Daily Southern Cross* of 6 December 1861 there was an article about one of the passengers on the *Gananoque* arriving at Auckland. His name was William Butcher and the ship's surgeon for the *Gananoque*, Mr. Cridges, testified that Butcher was an imbecile. Butcher unlawfully imported arms and ammunition that he had bought in London.

"William Butcher was then, brought forward on an indictment charging him with feloniously and unlawfully importing arms and ammunition, contrary to the provisions of the Arms' Act, 1860. Mr. Wynn (for the defence) demurred to this indictment, arguing that as the statute only made the offence charged a misdemeanour the use of the words "feloniously and unlawfully" gave a different character to the offence. This defect, he contended, was one of substance, which made against the entire indictment, and not surplussage merely which might be amended. The words also "imported from beyond the seas" were used in the indictment, but "from beyond the seas" were not in the statute. This was an additional objection to the indictment. Mr. Merriman replied, and contended that the use of the words "feloniously and unlawfully" did not necessarily constitute the offence a felony, seeing that the indictment set forth the offence, which the statute constituted a misdemeanour. The word, "feloniously" could only be looked upon as surplussage. After a few remarks from Mr. Wynn, The Chief Justice overruled the demurrer, but without prejudice to the prisoner should it afterwards appear to be one of substance. The prisoner was then formally arraigned, and pleaded not guilty to the charge. Mr. David Gomez Silva, officer of Customs, was examined, and deposed to the circumstances under which he seized the arms and ammunition of the prisoner in the *Gananoque* on the 21st; and 23rd October. He identified the property. Mr. Joseph Mohere Tabuteau, officer of Customs, proved that he had received the property identified by the last witness, and took possession of it on behalf of the Customs. Mr. Commissioner Naughton gave formal evidence. Mr. Cridges was examined. He deposed that he was surgeon of the *Gananoque* from London to Auckland. The prisoner was on board. On cross examination by Mr. Wynn, he swore that he considered the prisoner to be imbecile - a person of weak mind, not knowing what he did sometimes, but he would not say that he had no control over his own actions. In this transaction he believed the prisoner did not know what he was doing. Sergeant-Major Sims, of the police, was also examined to prove the identity of the property. In charging, the jury, his Honor raised the point-what was importation and remarked that it was a question for the jury, under the circumstances, whether the prisoner had in fact imported the arms and ammunition, or whether he had only been guilty of the intention. The jury found a verdict of guilty of the intent and his Honor, in passing sentence said it was apparent that the act was that of a rash young man, and the ends of justice would be satisfied by a sentence of one mouths' imprisonment, without hard labour, the prisoner having already been in jail from the 26th October. The prisoner made a statement regarding the manner of the purchase of the arms, which he said was from the first London houses. He had had £300 worth of jewellery, that had been taken from him, and which was worth £3,000 here, besides seven cases of goods which he had been deprived of altogether. On inquiry, it transpired that no goods belonging to the prisoner came by the *Gananoque* except the property produced: the jewellery seized was valued at £120. It was forfeited. This closed the business of the sessions."

Passengers on the Auckland Voyage
1861

Passengers on the Auckland Voyage 1861

Buchanan

George Buchanan was born in Scotland and came to New Zealand at the age of two on the *Gananoque* arriving in Auckland in 1861. George was educated in Auckland and served a jeweller's apprenticeship. He then set up his own business in Wellesley Street, Auckland before going into partnership with Mr. E. A. Price, trading under the name Buchanan and Co. The company became Buchanan and Co. Ltd. wholesale and manufacturing jewellers and was situated in Albert Street. He wound up the business shortly after WWI. He lived in Devonport, Auckland for 45 years. George was a member of the Artillery Band and of the "A" Battery Artillery. He was one of the leading members of the Devonport Bowling Club. George's wife died about ten years before his own death in 1931 at age 71. He was survived by his family of three sons, Edward, George and John, who all lived in Devonport, and five daughters. He was buried at O'Neill's Point Cemetery, Northshore, Auckland.[74]

Edmiston

James Edmiston was born in Paisley, Scotland, in about 1828. He came to Auckland on the ship *Gananoque* in 1861 with his wife Catherine and two children. He was the manager of Graham's Bond in Fort Street for many years and then of Firth's Bond. He was one of the earliest members of the Baptist Tabernacle, and was treasurer and collector of the building fund for many years. James was into bowls his whole life, including back in Scotland, and he was a member of the Ponsonby Bowling Club in Auckland. He was the treasurer of the club for many years and was a leading senior player. He was also in the Burns Club and the St. Andrew's Society. On James's death there was one son (Mr. H. J. Edmiston) and five daughters living, including Mrs. J. B. Thompson, Mrs. William, Mrs. Bernard Schmitt and Misses E., M., and L. Edmiston. James Edmiston passed away in 1912 at his house on Wood Street, Ponsonby, Auckland, aged 84.[75]

Nathan

Mr David Nathan founded a mercantile house called David Nathan and Co. in January 1840 at the same time as the proclamation of New Zealand as under British possession. He bought a quarter acre section in Shortland Street, Auckland at one of the first Government land sales and used it as the site of his business for the rest of his life. He also had a magnificent five-storey kauri gum and produce store in Customs and Commerce Streets, as well as a large tea warehouse in Customs Street, but these two buildings were destroyed in a massive fire in Auckland. His sons, Lawrence David Nathan and Nathan Alfred Nathan, took over the business calling it Nathan, L. D. and Co. They were wine and spirit and general merchants as well as shipping, fire and marine insurance agents and general produce brokers. They represented Shaw, Savill and Albion Co. Ltd. as shipping and marine insurance agents. In 1861 David Nathan and his family were returning from a voyage back to Great Britain. All the newspaper reports mention that he is on board the *Gananoque*, suggesting how highly respected he was. The two sons of David Nathan also owned an ostrich farm at Whitford Park. Lawrence and Nathan were keen sportsmen, and also bred famous New Zealand thoroughbred horses at their farm at Sylvia Park.[76]

Stichbury

James Stichbury was born in London in 1843 and travelled to New Zealand aboard the *Gananoque* in 1861. He came out under the charge of the late Mr David Nathan, who, in partnership with his uncle (Mr C. Stichbury) and Mr Jervis, was carrying on an auctioneering business under the style of David Nathan and Co. James had his first job working for Mr Nathan in Auckland but soon moved on to a job with Messrs J. S. Macfarlane and Co. and was then employed by Mr Ralph Keesing. James and his cousin then undertook a drapery business in Queen Street, which was interrupted in 1863 by military service, fighting

Mr. J. Stichbury

the Maori wars in the Waikato and Taranaki. James was enrolled in the first-class militia and worked his way up to the rank of sergeant. When the wars ended, James resumed business as an auctioneer in Queen Street. In 1867, the gold rush took him to Thames, where he had a business on Shortland Flat as a storekeeper, and then did some mining. He eventually returned to business in the city and was a salesman from 1875 to 1887 for Messrs S. Cochrane and Son, auctioneers. He then took on a business of general agent and valuer, which was his mainstay. James Stichbury was involved in the original Auckland Fire Brigade and belonged to the Order of Foresters. In 1894 he was an MP of the Ponsonby Ward in the City Council and also was involved with the Harbour Board. He was also a member of the District Hospital and Charitable Aid Board and was chairman for five years. He had a place of honour in connection with a Royal visit. His main local institution though was the Children's Hospital. James suggested that a separate, brighter hospital should be built as part of the Victoria Diamond Jubilee Memorial. He managed to get the Board to give £5000 of its quota to the hospital and it was the proudest day of his life when the foundation stone was laid.[77] James contested the mayoralty for Auckland in 1903 but didn't get voted in. He died in 1932 in his 90th year.[77]

Voyage to Port Chalmers, New Zealand

(7 December 1862 – 12 March 1863)

Voyage to Port Chalmers, New Zealand 1863

The *Gananoque* left Gravesend on 7 December 1862 for the third journey to New Zealand, with 91 passengers in total. There were 2 in the chief cabin, 20 passengers in second cabin and 69 in the steerage. Out of the steerage passengers, 47 were young females (including a lot of Irish girls). Including the second cabin passengers there were 29 males, 55 females and 5 children.

The diary of Alfred William Craymer lists about 29 of the passengers on the journey by name. See the passenger lists at the end of the book for a partial list of passengers on board this journey. There was no official passenger list surviving for this journey.

The ship left St Katharine's Docks, near Tower Bridge, London, for Gravesend, being towed by the steam tug *Britannia* on 6 December 1862. Family and friends waved them goodbye and the passengers returned the waves with handkerchiefs. This would likely be the last time they would see each other, a very sad time indeed for many. They arrived at Gravesend at 5pm and had some dinner of fresh boiled beef, soup and bread, which was described as "pretty good." This would not be the case with all meals on board however.

The next day some of the passengers disembarked, had a meal at Gravesend and purchased a few things that they discovered they needed for the journey. The Inspector came on board and called for changes to be made before the journey could proceed, including moving the passengers' luggage out of wet conditions and also providing the passengers with more light.

On 7 December 1862, Mr. Savill (presumably of Shaw, Savill & Co.) and his clerk came on board the ship, and Captain David Ritchie was also walking around. The anchor was weighed at 12 o'clock, the mainsail unfurled and they were officially off on their adventure. The winds were unfavourable though so they anchored near the Nore, a sandbank at the mouth of the Thames estuary.

On 8 December, they set sail for the Downs. Some of the ladies were starting to "feed the fishes" as the 23 year old diary writer Alfred William Craymer put it, vomiting over the side. Even Alfred himself felt rather "dicky." The provisions such as bread, tea, coffee, sugar and mustard and three quarts of water each daily were served out. Provisions on this journey were always served out on a Monday. It was a fine sunny day and a very enjoyable voyage for the passengers. Then when they anchored in the Downs the sea was quite rough and most passengers were trying not to be sick and keeping near an appropriate place to do so.

On Tuesday 9 December, a flag was hoisted to indicate to the shore for a boat to come out with supplies. They (presumably Alfred and his mates) purchased beer and herrings. Alfred was travelling with his friends Mr. Watters and Mr. Mitchell. They also had others in their cabin, including Dr Corse and a Mr Gellatly from Scotland, who had lived quite a while in America and knew all about the Civil War there. There was a small wrestling match between Watters and a Mr Savage, with the later winning. They sighted about 300 ships near Deal and also a large pod of porpoises. It started raining and blowing hard, and the ship started dragging its anchor which necessitated 180 feet more cable being let out.

Over the next two days the sea was very rough and they beat down the English Channel with the passengers very ill indeed. The sight of the sails of many ships took Alfred's breath away. He noticed that they were all heading in the same direction and then suddenly all took their own route out to sea, heading on their own long journeys around the world. A truly romantic sight!

On Friday 12 December, they were off the Isle of Wight with about two or three other ships. Alfred had a verbal fight with the Second Mate after he ordered Alfred around. Alfred didn't like this as the crew member was a mere lad. Alfred and Watters threatened to throw him overboard and he ended up apologising.

On Saturday 13 December, the sea was huge and most of the passengers went back to bed due to illness. Massive waves broke over the ship causing tin cans to fly about. They spoke the *Belmont* going from London to the East Indies. Alfred commented that he did not feel like writing a letter home as he was too ill.

They had two services on Sunday 14 December, a Scottish and an

English service, both officiated by a Mr Lawton. They were sitting off the Cornish coast and the sea was dead calm. Everyone breathed a sigh of relief.

On Monday they sighted the schooner *La Cruz*. The boat came up alongside and they exchanged numbers. They were now in the Atlantic and England was being left behind. Many of the passengers would never see their homeland again. Because they were now in the open ocean, the anchors were drawn up and fastened on the forecastle and cable chains put in a box. Then the decks were all cleaned and it appeared to the passengers that there was more room now.

On Tuesday, Alfred got up early and went on deck to a lovely morning's weather. He felt really good. Gellatly baked a cake and it was devoured with much gusto. Alfred thought it would "open the Ladies' eyes" to see men making cakes! At night he "went home" which meant going to his cabin and bunk, which he said was just great. He played whist (a card game), sung "John Barley Corn" with his cabin mates and generally had a good time. Late at night the sea got very rough and the water cans were flying about in the neighbour's cabin, waking poor Alfred up.

On Thursday 18 December, they were skirting the Bay of Biscay and the climate felt much warmer. Alfred played a game of draughts, losing to Dr. Corse, and smoked his first ever cigar. He also turned down an offer to write an article for a newspaper called the *Gananogue* (this is how Alfred spelt the ship's name). Alfred could see it being a flop, and it was. That night the ship got a burst of wind and was travelling at the rate of 12 knots. It made everyone happy and lively.

On Friday, Captain Ritchie got more sails up; 21 sails total by Alfred's count. They were cutting through the water almost imperceptibly. At 12 o'clock the fore studding sail boom was snapped "like...a match" by a sudden gust of wind. This didn't seem to be a major problem. Alfred was told that most ships expected to lose a studding sail boom or two while at sea. Porpoises were racing the ship. They were more likely to appear when it was a strong breeze.

On Saturday 20 December, Alfred fell in his cabin and sprained his hip. He talks a lot about people falling head over heels on deck or inside the ship, due to the movement. He felt sore for days afterwards. He got a carpenter on board to make him a knife box and he assisted. There were quite a few homeward-bound ships in sight but they were too far away to be spoken with.

On Sunday they had the usual services and Mitchell's 32nd birthday was celebrated. Porpoises were again around the ship and the men tried to harpoon one but without success.

Then it was Monday and the provisions were handed out, but the Third Mate was, in some cases, dishing out under half what was allowed, especially to the girls on board. There were complaints to the Captain and he made the Third Mate weigh everything out correctly.

On Tuesday 23 December, they sighted Madeira through the haze. The girls had a dress competition but Alfred thought it was like a "rag shop" or "Petticoat Lane." Obviously the dresses were not very fine. He played whist and quoits that he and his cabin mates had made using rope from the ship, and there was a wrestling match. Later Alfred came on deck to listen to the flute being played. Jack (a sailor) and other sailors then engaged in lively and inspiring singing which made everyone happy.

On Christmas Day 1862, the passengers had plain plum pudding, but Alfred said it was sufficient. The crew were all on deck extremely drunk and were quarrelling with the cooks but eventually things calmed down. There was some dancing on deck, but Alfred called Christmas day "tame." He said, though, that under the circumstances it wasn't too bad. The next day there were many sick people on board and the healthy ones went to see who had overdone it. That night there was more singing and dancing until 9pm.

On Saturday 27 December, the sea was like a millpond. They were in the tropics and it was very misty. They travelled at 6 knots per hour. The Dr started to fall for a girl named Alice Wade and everyone noticed! On Sunday they saw several flying fish. Alfred described them as the size of a herring, leaping a short distance out of the water and under again. A man went up the foremast to look out for land as they were in the latitude of the Cape de Verde Islands (now Cape Verde). The Dr and Alice Wade sat together most of the day, but once he went to bed Paterson took over! Oh the charms of fair Alice!

On Monday 29 December they were 120 miles south of the Cape de Verde Islands. Some of the men cut each other's hair, not very successfully. It was so hot that many passengers left off their stockings and socks.

The Doctor had a bath on Tuesday, which meant buckets of water were drawn up from the sea and thrown over him. Being hot, it would have been not too unpleasant. They saw more flying fish. Alfred was very hot and drank his lime juice which he said is quite nice when sugar is added.

Sailfin flying-fish (Wikipedia)

On New Year's Eve, the scotch came out and everyone got merry, including Alfred who said it was only once a year. It was a very lively day and Alfred stayed up until 12am to see in the New Year. One can only imagine the shenanigans on board that day.

On New Year's Day, the wind was light and the ship was in the variables. A pig had a fit and was killed by one of the butchers on board. Alfred didn't like the meat and preferred the salt junk (salted meat). It rained very hard in the afternoon and they caught 500 gallons of rainwater in barrels for washing in which was much better than washing in salty sea water. The stored fresh water on board was only for drinking.

Alfred had his first good wash or "ablutions," as he called it, because the ship was becalmed. This was on 2 January, almost a month after leaving port. Washing properly only once a month must have meant a great stench of unwashed bodies onboard. One can just imagine it!

The girls did a lot of washing too that day. The rainwater they had caught was a "godsend." Alfred saw a portuguese-man-of-war, which is probably the jellyfish of this name. He said it was also called a nautilus, but the two animals are completely different. It was most likely a jellyfish floating on the top of the water.

On 3 January, it was still raining, as it had done the day before. They saw a homeward-bound ship but couldn't speak to them as they were too far away. The Doctor and Alfred did their washing but it all got wet while hanging to dry outside.

The next day Alfred collected his clothes which had been out all night and they were nice and dry. The Scottish and English services were held. A bird called a whale bird landed on deck and couldn't rise again, so was caught. Eventually they set it free again. Alfred says, "Sun set magnificent and Moon as clear as crystal. It is impossible for me in words to describe the beauty of either as seen at sea in the tropics."

On 5 January, a sailor named Jack Allen harpooned a porpoise and on trying to get it on board it got a half foot long gash in its back. It was a terrible sight. The animal managed to get away and had a tremendous fall back into the water and then darted away but the other porpoises were chasing after it, smelling its blood. Alfred thought they were going to eat him but they were probably protecting the injured animal. Also the whale bird from the previous day landed on deck again and was caught and kept in the second cabin for quite a while.

On Tuesday 6 January, they crossed the line (Equator) at 26° W[78] and shaving was organised for the crew (see later in the book for particulars). Also a shark came alongside the ship and the crew tried to harpoon it without success.

The next day they spoke the Prussian brig *Popplewell*. Everyone was hopeful they could send letters home but not on this ship. That night they baked some bread and had some songs from the sailors.

The ship was becalmed again on 8 January, which was very tiring for the passengers. They washed in fresh water – a real treat, and Jack Allen, the sailor, went for a swim in the sea, but wouldn't let go of the rope for fear of the shark they had seen.

The next day they met the South East trades and had a strong breeze taking them at a rate of 9 knots towards South America. There was a ship ahead of them, but they were gaining on it very fast. The weather was incredibly hot. Alfred had on a calico cap made by one of the girls on board, as his black hat was attracting the heat too much. The ship from the previous day was spoken with on 10 January and it was *Iris* from Oporto to Rio Grande. They passed the ship and were travelling at 10 knots. There was dancing that night and Alice Wade danced with Mr Stott, leaving the Doctor with no dance partner. He went to bed instead.

Ascension Island. Creative Commons Attribution 3.0 Licence

On 11 January, the *Gananoque* was about 9.43° S latitude, 23.39° W longitude, not too far from Ascension Island, but it was not in view. The girls on board were being a bit loose for Alfred's taste and were kissing the men on board. Maybe the Matron was not doing her job properly that day!

The next day the crew set about catching a thief onboard. The thieving sailor got the lesson of his life when he stole bread that had jalap (a purgative drug) inserted into the middle. The bread passed through him quickly as well as through the sailor's lover. A quick and easy way to find out who the thief was!

On Wednesday 14 January, they saw a ship sailing for the United Kingdom but were too far away to speak or to give letters to them. So the letters were put away and everyone was disappointed. Alfred had peeling skin and said he was "as brown as sugar." It was very hot. The next day they were at latitude 19.26° S. There was a water fight and they all ran to avoid detection by the crew, but Alfred slipped and had internal pains through the night. The next day he was still in pain. They were at latitude 20.44° S and the heat was so tremendous the tar was running down the rigging in icicles, and on deck the pitch was boiling and easily stuck to the passengers' feet.

Albatross – A 1837 Woodcut from the journal "O Panorama". Creative Commons Attribution 3.0 Licence

On 17 January, three ships were in sight at latitude 22.37° S, but they couldn't send their letters. The next day they caught a fish called "Bonita" (probably an Atlantic bonito) and it was soon devoured.

19 January it was quite squally but cleared up in the evening. The next day the ship was becalmed and there wasn't much happening. A passenger climbed the rigging and was strapped there by the crew and ordered to pay with alcohol. This occurred a couple of times during the journey.

By 22 January the passengers all seemed tired of the voyage. They hadn't been on land for one and a half months. They were only halfway through the voyage and already the medical supplies were exhausted. If anyone had actually got seriously ill they would probably have died, unless Dr Corse could have found a remedy!

The ship was at 29.19° S on 23 January. They only travelled 78 miles that day. Two days later they were at 32.55° S and rain started to come down from 4pm. On 26 January, Alfred saw some cape hens and albatross, and hoped to catch one of them as the wing spans were about 15 to 17 feet across. The next day they were at 34.59° S and 18° W and the ship was rolling from side to side with some passengers "casting up accounts," as Alfred wrote.

Sperm whaling c.1850s. Creative Commons Attribution 3.0 Licence

On 28 January, hooks were put out with pork on them for catching albatross. A small one was caught but set free again. The passengers wanted to bring up guns for cleaning but the Captain wouldn't allow shooting on board. What a wise man! They had 200 to 300 sperm whales around the ship, all spouting and looking like ships. Some were the size of the *Gananoque* itself! The passengers, who seemed to like to kill everything, even thought about harpooning one, but soon changed their minds.

The next day Alfred mentioned that "time seems to hang heavy." The journey was painfully slow. They were at 35.51° S. Then on 30 January the passengers hurried up on deck to see the magnificent sight of Tristan da Cunha, an island with a mountainous peak. Alfred commented that it was 6400 feet above sea level. The ship was at 37.6° S latitude and 12.6 ° W longitude. They were 15 miles West South West of the island. Alfred had never heard of it in his life. It was 1 February and Alfred had put on a collar and scarf as he was cold. He hadn't worn them for six weeks. The next day Alfred and his mates wanted spirit to "warm the cockles" but couldn't get it from the third mate, so they asked the Captain who "promised to see about it." They got their rum the next day and were at 40.39° S.

On Wednesday 4 February Alfred wrote: "Arose at 6 fine morning, steady breeze while walking on the starboard deck a young woman asked me to draw her up a bucket of water and of course with my usual willingness to do what I can to oblige the Ladies I readily complied and presented her with the bucket of water (sea water) while occupied, the conversation was most interesting to me she anxiously enquired how I had slept last night and significantly said she had been dreaming of me all night, poor Dear thought I and said ironically, "how strange I have been dreaming of your also." this put her heart into a flutter and she fluttered away (Just Fancy)."

The same day Jack Allen came to the pumps, drunk and started singing indecent songs, which the Captain ordered the Boatswain to put a stop to, but a fight ensued. Jack went for the Captain a couple of times and nearly ended up in irons. The sailors all were drunk because passengers had given them drink, but luckily the breeze was strong enough that they were not needed. The Richmond brothers had given the sailors the booze and had got drunk themselves.

Alfred hoped he would never hear such bad language again as from those men. And as he put it "they were soon wrapped in deep sleep but only to continue a noise equally as unpleasant as the others, only in a different key – very few of us got rest this night . . ."

Two days later the ship wasn't moving. One of the girls on board was very ill and was not expected to live. On 7 February they were at 44.56° S latitude and then at 45.18° S the next day. On 9 February preparations were being made for Valentine's Day on board the ship. The Carpenter's house was going to be the Post Office and Alfred and his mate Watters were selecting and composing poetry to send to the girls. Some were nice poems praising the girls and some the opposite! Alfred was asked to write something for a girl Mary Anne Smith. She obviously couldn't write, yet wanted to send something home to family. He wrote, "the Sun would rise tomorrow in the North after dinner and set at 10o'C at night also that we had seen several large fish called albatross in the south and several large birds called porpoises." Alfred was a cheeky rascal. Mr. Stott has fallen "head over heels" with Alice Wade and the Doctor no longer has a chance with her, it seems. Also, a pig was killed that day.

10 February and they are at 47.5° S latitude and 31° E longitude. Alfred stayed up until 12am reading a book on New Zealand but said "a great deal of it is very different in reality to what is represented therein." Also the girl who was ill had recovered and could now come on deck. Two days later, they sighted Marion Island and Prince Edward Island, sailing about 23 miles to the south of them.

On 13 February, Alfred had received about 80 Valentine's messages in the post office but said "as soon as it is dark expect a lot more as those Dear Creatures do not like to be seen putting the letters in box." The wind had increased a great deal and all the royals were taken in as well as the cross jack mizzen, the foretopgallant sails and mainsail.

It was Valentine's Day. There were about 150 Valentines received and the Carpenter was postman. The ladies were extremely excited. Captain Ritchie and the First Mate enjoyed it. Some people received abusive Valentines and accused Alfred of it, which he was very unhappy about. One lady sent Alfred a Valentine and said she loved him but she would love him more if it wasn't for his "winking eyes." A sheep was killed that day "to save its life," as Alfred wrote.

On 16 February they were at latitude 47.21° S and longitude 56° E which meant they had made good progress, but Alfred uses the word "dull" a lot - dull dinner of junk, potatoes and rice and dull weather too. Many of the cabin passengers accused Alfred of sending them Valentines but he said it wasn't him. They were probably not very nice Valentines.

Christmas Harbour, Kerguelens Land by George Cooke, 1811. Creative Commons Attribution 3.0 Licence

On 18 February, the ship was at 47.4° S as Captain Ritchie thought they would get stronger winds there, but Alfred said that later on he had to go further south. The passengers played Judge and Jury, as they must have been getting very bored. They pretended there was a case of sheep stealing and had a whole court case. They had generally had light weather up until this point of the journey.[78] On Friday 20 February they passed Kerguelen Islands but kept well north and, because of the fog, didn't sight them. The ship's medicine chest was completely exhausted and Alfred commented that the medical check at Gravesend was a complete farce. They had some dancing that night. The next day it rained and the sea was tremendously wild. It came on in a hurry.

On 24 February, they were at 47.9° S latitude and 92° E longitude. The rain continued, and on the 25th it was extremely wild and Alfred says that the "tremendous seas are drawing nearly everyone and everything on deck." Two albatrosses were caught and killed and Watters got the head and wing of one, as a souvenir. Alfred describes the storm so wonderfully that one can imagine being there:

"After tea I was on deck standing amidships and looking upon one of the most glorious sights I ever saw yet awful indeed waves like mountain rising behind and before us and the gallant vessel leaping as it were into the air right over them and sinking down on their crests – going from her course and every rope and sail stretched to its tightest when suddenly the Starboard main Pack chain broke and the thick rope struck me and sent me rolling flung me up against the pig sty but fortunately did not hurt me much had the running block to which the chain was attached hit me I should either have been killed or maimed for life after this."

The women were all downstairs during the storm and most of the Irish girls were praying for their lives. The storm went through the night and the gale increased further still. The wheel was lashed to the bulwarks to prevent the *Gananoque* from drifting. The next day the storm abated somewhat and by 27 February they were at latitude 49.18° S and longitude 101° E. They had very cold weather for a few days and Alfred spent time in bed in the daytime. On 2 March they were at latitude 49.42° S and longitude 118° E, below Australia.

On 5 March, they were at 122° E, longitude and a day later at 48.57° S latitude and 135.30 ° E longitude. They were travelling fast. That day the First Mate was being particularly gracious and Alfred said he knew what he was up to – he wanted the passengers to write a favourable testimonial. These sometimes ended up in the local paper. On 6 March they were at 49.17° S and 149° E. A pig was killed. There was magnificent moonlight which apparently indicated land was near!

On Sunday 8 March, there was sunshine but a rough sea, and it was striking the *Gananoque* and making things fly about. The passengers could hardly stand up. One girl ended up falling down the poop ladder and another girl was struck by a wave and "lifted from Port side to Starboard side clean over Hatchway." It was certainly a very dangerous day to be walking around on deck. The *Gananoque* were at 48.45° S latitude 154.25° E longitude. The next day Alfred packed up his things, ready for disembarking.

On Tuesday 10 March, they sighted a barque heading for the North Island and were at latitude 47.35° and longitude 165.55° E. At 4 pm they sighted the Snares - rocky islands south of New Zealand.

On 11 March, they sighted New Zealand for the first time. They also saw a barque going up the mouth of the Clutha River. The *Gananoque* sailed up the coast all day; "hugging the land." At 6pm they were off Nugget Point and Molyneux Bay. By 8 am the next morning they were close to Port Chalmers and the Pilot soon boarded the *Gananoque*. The steam tug *Samson* took them into Port Chalmers which took about two hours. Alfred said "the scenery here was delightful and the harbour most intricate and winding." Most of the passengers left the ship the next day to start their new life in New Zealand.

Peculiar facts from the journey

Telling the Time

At sea there was an unusual way of telling the time and a bell was struck as follows:

> 8 times at 4 o'clock and 1 times for 4.30
> 2 times at 5 o'clock and 3 times for 5.30
> 4 times at 6 o'clock and 5 times for 6.30
> 6 times at 7 o'clock and 7 times for 7.30
> 8 times at 8 o'clock etc.

Spoke a ship – what does this entail?

In newspaper reports of ships it often said the "*Gananoque* spoke the *Popplewell*" and so on. What does this mean? Alfred comments that if you see a homeward bound ship you signal them with your number in flags (each vessel has a number, which is represented by flags placed in different ways). Often the ships would exchange food and take letters back home from passengers. Of course, the ship had to be close enough to do all of this.

Mending ropes etc.

Alfred mentioned the sailors mending the ropes and tarring them. When they are in hot conditions the tar melts and the thick ropes are easily bent. The heavy sails are hauled out to see if they have been rubbed and this is usually done in calm weather.

Preparations for shaving once Equator is crossed

This seems to happen on most ships when the Equator is crossed (called "crossing the line"). The day before the line was crossed the sailors of the *Gananoque* prepared a tar barrel with tar and straw inside for the event.

Next, a group of people stood on the forecastle. They represented Neptune. Neptune yelled "Hello." A reply of "What Oh" came back from others on the ship. Neptune then asked the people a series of questions such as the name of the ship, where they have come from, how long out from port and how many people on board. Then Neptune said he would come and visit again tomorrow. The tar barrel was then lit and thrown overboard so it could be seen as a small light for miles and miles. It rose and fell with the waves.

The next day the *Gananoque* crossed the line and one sailor who had never crossed the line before got pulled into the shaving palaver. He had to sit on a chair while a sail was spread from the bulwarks on the leeward side of the ship over to a lifeboat. They then used the ship's pump to fill the sail with water. Everyone wore silly clothes. Some of the sailors were wearing girls' clothes. Then they lathered up the guys face with tar and used hoop iron for the razor. The sailor was blindfolded during the whole thing. They asked him questions but if the sailor answered properly he would get pills and other things thrown in his mouth and pushed down with a tar brush. Luckily he knew not to answer the questions and kept his mouth shut. They then threw the sailor into the sail and got him wet, all the crew getting wet as well. The pump was then used and water squirted from the hose into the unsuspecting passengers. Pails of water were thrown over people and many looked like drowned rats. Most of the passengers enjoyed the celebrations and getting so wet!

Food – including rat and maggot pea soup!

Just about every single meal is noted in the ship's diary, some good meals and some very bad.

Alfred loved his bergoo, which was a kind of porridge. He and some others became known as the "Bergoo Jammers" as they really enjoyed their almost daily bergoo!

Some of the sheep that were slaughtered for food were in very poor condition and Alfred wouldn't eat them. He even preferred the salt junk sometimes (salted meat). For some reason rice was called "strike the blind" by the sailors.

The worst meal was near the end of the journey when Alfred noticed rice added to the pea soup. On closer inspection they found it was maggots and that they were all through the soup. A rat was later found in a girl's hook pot – a very large and decomposing rat, full of maggots, which had somehow fallen into the boiler. At least the soup was well boiled to kill any germs. Alfred joked that the girl had extra meat to add to the pork at dinner time.

Animals seen and killed

The passengers were obsessed with killing anything they could get their hands on. This was good for food in some cases, but also there seemed to be a barbaric streak running through some of the passengers who were looking for souvenirs. Maybe it was boredom that drove them to do it, or maybe it was the way things were in 1863. They maimed a dolphin, which got away and probably died. Two albatross were divided up into body parts for souvenirs. Fish and sharks were caught or harpooned for much needed fresh food, although the sharks kept getting away. Cape pigeons were also the target of the hunt, but the diary doesn't mention any being caught.

Rats in the kid boots

The ship was plagued by rats, as Alfred and his cabin mates could hear them squeaking and moving around at night while they tried to sleep. The baby rats were "squealing, near West's Head," as he put it. Alfred nearly had a lovely pair of spring kid boots spoiled and he thought only one more night of them feasting on them and they would have only been worth throwing in the rubbish.

The Arrival of the *Gananoque*

The *Otago Daily Times* reports that on arrival on the 12 March 1863 the *Gananoque* had 91 passengers on board. [78]

Alice Wade and Joseph Ebenezer Stott had a very interesting onboard romance. During the voyage they sat next to each other at the Sunday English services and seemed very pleased with each other's company. Alice had also been the receiver of attention from Dr Corse. He was very downhearted when Stott took over as the main love interest. Dr Corse's cabin mates noticed his disappointment. Then a Mr Paterson tried to get her attention as well, but Mr Stott was still the main love interest.

It appears that Alice and Joseph stayed together. They married in 1863, not long after arrival in New Zealand and had a daughter Alice Dale Stott born in 1864. They travelled back to Great Britain on a mail steamer leaving 18 July 1865.[79] Maybe colonial life was not to their liking? They appeared in the 1881 census in Edinburgh, Scotland, living at 60 St Marys Street. Joseph had set himself up as a confectioner and the family had expanded to four children including: Alice Dale, 17, Amelia, 14, Mary W., 12 and John W., 10.

There were no births or deaths on the voyage and Alfred Craymer doesn't mention any marriages.

After offloading the cargo, the *Gananoque* set sail on 4 May 1863 for Guam, in ballast. The agent was Dalgety, Rattray & Co.[80]

The Fate of the Single Women

In a letter to the editor, written the day after the *Gananoque* arrived, was a big discussion about what happened to the single women arriving at Port Chalmers. Miss Maria Rye discussed how hard it was for single women on the sea voyage having single men on the same ship, especially if you had an incompetent matron and a drunk captain. And once the cry of "land ahoy" had been made most women felt so relieved and observed the colours and smells of their new land with pure delight. This excitement was shattered however as the women disembarked and entered the Dunedin Immigrant's Barracks. They were sleeping not far from men of the Otago constabulary who occupied half the building. They had no drinking water and had to walk to a public house to get a simple drink and there was nowhere to wash after a four month sea journey. There was no bench to sit on and no table on which to place food. It was also an immoral place with prostitution going on in full view. There were two or three single mothers living there and a few waiting to give birth!

However, for an independent and moral woman who wanted to make a go of it, then New Zealand was the place to go. Females were highly sought after for work. A governess, who had just arrived, could get a wage of £40 to £60 per annum. A domestic servant could receive £20 to £40 pounds per annum. As discussed earlier in this book, the average wage in the United Kingdom for a housemaid in the 1850s and 1860s was £11 to £14. Things in New Zealand at that time were more expensive though, due to it being a new land. Produce was especially dear, but wages reflected this.[32]

The single women arriving on the *Gananoque,* including lots of Irish girls, were sent to the barracks at Dunedin. They would have had an hour-long journey on a steamer and then arrived at a jetty, where an immigration officer would have met them and walked them to the barracks. Hopefully it would have only taken them a few days to get new positions in their new land, and create happy and exciting new lives for themselves, full of opportunities.

We have to draw the attention of those requiring domestic servants to the notice in another column that the female immigrants who have arrived by the Gananoque are ready to receive engagements. Application must be made to the matron at the Immigration Barracks between the hours of 10 and 4.

Otago Daily Times 17 March 1863

NOW BEING LANDED,

EX "GANANOQUE,"

EVERY REQUISITE IN BABY LINEN

AND

LADIES' UNDERCLOTHING.

—

HERBERT, HAYNES, & HAY,

Princes-street,

Near the Octagon.

Otago Daily Times, 28 March 1863

Gananoque Cargo 1863

Per Gananoque, from London : 40 hhds, Tickle and Co ; 6 packages, 1 case, order ; 26 packages, W and G Turnbull and Co ; 36 cases, order ; 1 case, Berg, Christie and Co ; 20 barrels, order ; 2 cases, Julius Vogel ; 100 packages, Morison, Law and Co ; 4 cases, order ; 58 packages, J and J H Barr ; 1 case, J Jones and Co ; 1 qr-cask, Captain Boyd ; 12 packages, Kingston ; 4 cases, A Silvester ; 2 cases, Dalgety, Rattray and Co ; 12 trunks, Morrison, Law and Co ; 20 cases, order ; 5 packages, J Preston ; 2 cases, A H Sherry ; 2 cases, 30 hhds, order ; 4 casks, J Reid ; 63 pkgs, Herbert, Haynes and Hay ; 51 pkgs F Barker ; 3 cases, H Nathan ; 1 case, Cargill & Co ; 10 pkgs, H Nathan ; 10 cases, order ; 1 case, W and G Turnbull and Co ; 18 packages. J Brown ; 20 packages, D R Girdwood ; 1 case, Bing and Co ; 10 packages, order : 10 packages, J Jones and Co : 50 hhds. Morrison, Law and Co ; 132 packages, Tickle and Co ; 55 packages. Dalgety, Rattray and Co ; 22 boxes, T Ancell ; 67 packages, Day and Mieville ; 80 packages. J Finch and Co ; 215 packages, order ; 965 packages, 51 cases, Dalgety, Rattray and Co ; 3 cases, J Moss ; 50 tons coal. 25 packages, Dalgety, Rattray and Co ; 17 cases, order ; 126 packages, 9 cases, 1 bale, W and G Turnbull and Co ; 24 cases. H Kirkpatrick ; 60 cases, Franck and Co ; 15 packages. 1 case, Murray. Kerr and Co ; 9 packages, J Ross ; 420 packages, order : 1 box, Dobbie and Co : 2,121 packages, 17,424 fire bricks, order ; 746 packages, Cargill and Co ; 5 packages, W G Turnbull and Co ; 8 packages, Franck and Co ; 24 packages. order ; 10 packages, Murray, Kerr and Co ; 645 packages, Robinson, Hart and Co ; 60 packages, J Kohn and Co ; 246 packages, Murray, Kerr and Co ; 24 packages, W and G Turnbull and Co ; 34 packages, H Nathan ; 3 cases, order.

List of Cargo on the Gananoque, Otago Daily Times 13 March 1863

Map of the Journey of the *Gananoque* 1863

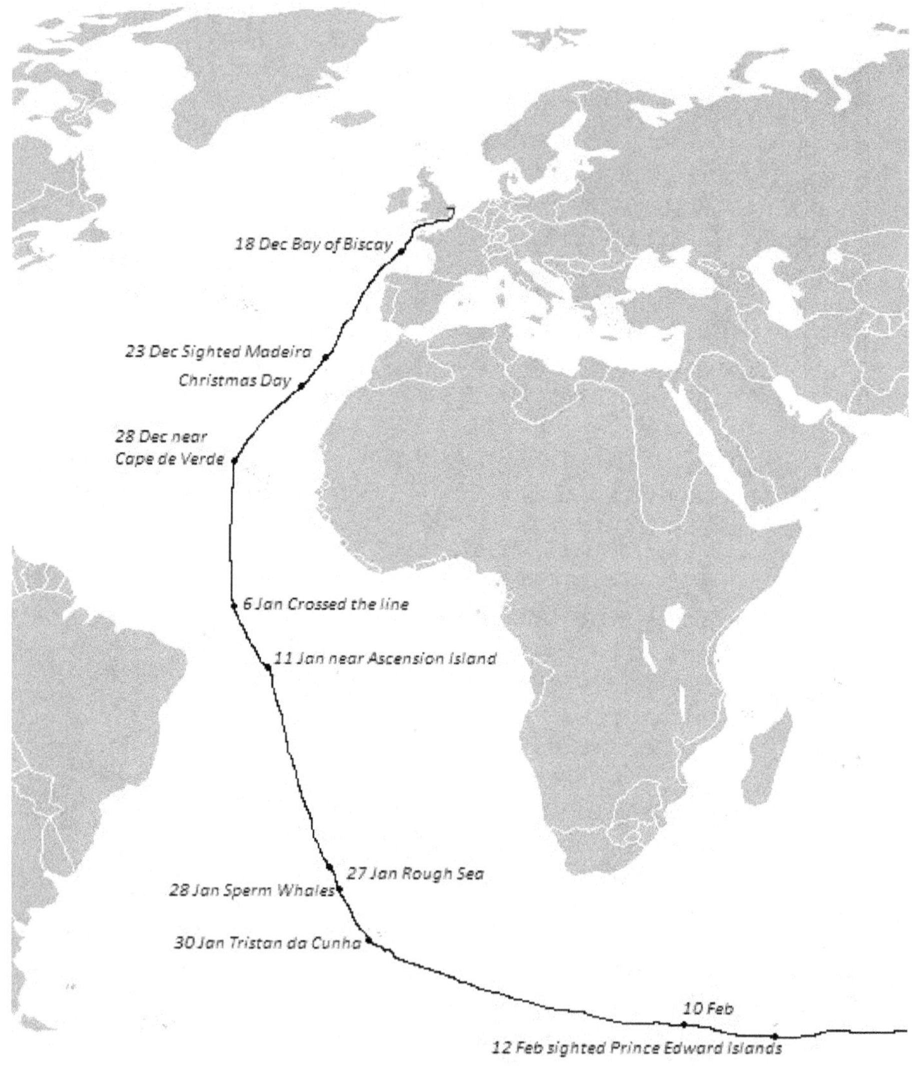

(7 December 1862 – 12 March 1863)

Passengers on the Port Chalmers Voyage 1863

Passengers on the Port Chalmers Voyage 1863

Caird

George Caird was born in Arbroath, Scotland in about 1842. He was an apprentice to his father G. Caird in Arbroath and completed this apprenticeship in 1860. George travelled to New Zealand on the *Gananoque,* landing at Port Chalmers and then travelled to the goldfields of Westland, where he mined for seven years. After this, he moved to Canterbury, where he spent fourteen years. According to the Cyclopedia of New Zealand, George's "career in the colonies has been fairly successful." He travelled a lot and knew a lot about the "most startling incidents" in early New Zealand history.   He finally settled in Palmerston North and became a general storekeeper in Main Street. He was a elected to a seat on the Palmerston North Borough Council in 1896.[81]   In 1866, George married Isabella McDonald in Matau, Inchclutha, Otago. They had eight children in total, three boys and five girls. Isabella died in 1921 in Wanganui. George died in 1922 in Wanganui. Both were buried in Aramoho Cemetery, Wanganui, New Zealand.[82]

Coleman

Mary Ann Coleman was born in Boyle, County Roscommon, Ireland in 1842. She was the daughter of Dominic Coleman and Mary McHugh. She travelled to New Zealand on board the *Gananoque* in 1863, arriving at Port Chalmers. She married Nicholas Smith, a labourer/stevedore, in Dunedin in 1864.[83] Nicholas and Mary had six children named John, Louisa, Cornelius, Andrew James, Ernest and Kate Maria. Louisa Smith married Thomas Ryan, a fireman on board the ship *Wairarapa*, and travelled over to Sydney in 1894 with her mother Mary Ann, after Nicholas Smith died in August 1894. Both Mary Ann and Louisa perished after the *Wairarapa* struck Great Barrier Island out from Auckland, but Thomas Ryan survived the *Wairarapa* tragedy. He joined the NZ Police and did wonderful service, saving many lives.[84]

Craymer

Alfred William Craymer was born in 1840 in London, England. He travelled to Port Chalmers, New Zealand in 1863 on board the *Gananoque* and wrote the only known ship's diary for the vessel's journeys to New Zealand. After arriving, he married Eugenia Jones in 1867 at St Paul's Church, Dunedin. Eugenia had been living in Breadalbane, near Goulburn, New South Wales, Australia but was originally from London. They had at least one child in New Zealand named Percy Alfred Craymer, born 1869. It appears they then moved to Australia.

Stevenson

Margaret Stevenson was born in Banff, Scotland 24 October 1841, daughter of John Stevenson and Janet Scott. She arrived in Dunedin, New Zealand on board the *Gananoque*. She married John Middleton Collie in Dunedin in 1863 and they lived in different parts of New Zealand including Dunedin, Wellington and Upper Hutt. They had several children. She died on 4 October 1907.[85]

Voyage to Southland, New Zealand

(16 May 1864 – 5 September 1864)

Voyage to Southland, New Zealand 1864

The *Gananoque* made one final journey to New Zealand departing 16 May 1864 and arriving at Port of Bluff Harbour on 5 September 1864.

The Commander was again Captain David Ritchie, on a second journey out to New Zealand. The journey was a cargo journey only, with no passengers on board. The ship brought a large cargo with a lot of railway plant for the Government.[86] There was a very long description of the journey in the *Southland Times* of 6 September 1864, which details the route taken. They had moderately fine weather for the whole passage.

The *Gananoque* left London on 16 May and passed through the Downs on 17 May. On the 21 May it passed the Scilly Islands off the coast of Cornwall.

The *Gananoque* met with a great number of ships on the journey. On 19 June at latitude 41° N, longitude 21.45° W they spoke the *Regina,* which was travelling from London to Melbourne. Three days later, on 21 June, they crossed the Equator at 26° W longitude.

They exchanged numbers with the *Palmerston* from Cardiff to Shanghai on 27 June. On 30 June, they exchanged numbers with the ship *Robert Lees,* which was travelling from London to Calcutta. The *Robert Palsford* was the next ship they exchanged numbers with, on 11 July, which was travelling from Liverpool to Calcutta. On 16 July, they exchanged numbers with the French ship *St. Louis* from Bordeaux to Melbourne, at latitude 36.53° S, longitude 35° E. The next day they exchanged numbers with a Dutch barque called *Mentor* travelling from Amsterdam to Padang at latitude 36.56° S, longitude 53.7° E. On 2 August, they exchanged numbers with the *Morning Star* travelling from London to Sydney at latitude 45.56° S longitude 60.3° E. They exchanged numbers on 5 August with the *Mirage* travelling from London to Canterbury, New Zealand at latitude 46.10° S, longitude 71.28° E. On 26 August, they spoke the Oldenburg ship *Atlas* from London to Wellington at latitude 47.16° S and longitude 146.23° E.[87]

The *Gananoque* arrived at the Port of Bluff Harbour at 8 pm on 5 September 1864..

The only other interesting thing about this journey was that one of the seamen, Richard Coutes, deserted the ship and was charged on 20 October 1864. He was sentenced to six weeks imprisonment with hard labour and 40 shillings to be taken from his wages to pay for expenses.[88]

According to the newspapers, *Gananoque* left Port of Bluff Harbour for Singapore on 31 October 1864, in ballast, with McPherson and Co, agents.[89] The journey had a few more stops however. After leaving the Port of Bluff they stopped at Hong Kong, Manila, Puget Sound and China before landing at Singapore. Then the boat continued to London via the island of Mauritius.[90]

Map of the Journey of the *Gananoque* 1864

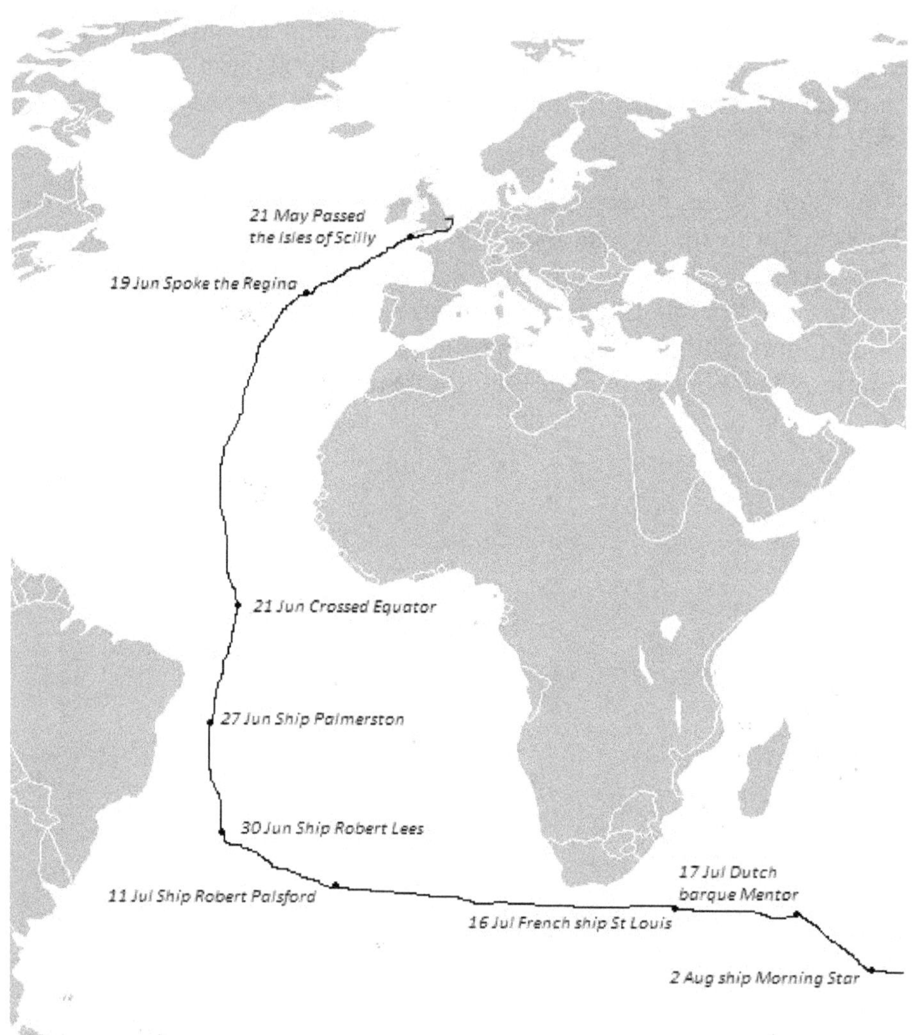

(16 May 1864 – 5 September 1864)

Passenger Lists

The 1860 list has been transcribed directly from the passenger lists of steerage passengers, with cabin passengers taken from newspaper articles. Corrections were made after research was done on the passengers. The original transcriptions are in square brackets beside the correct spelling. There may still be errors in the list which render some names too different to the real people who landed in New Zealand. The 1861 list has been completely taken from newspapers as no hand written passenger list exists. This means there may be many errors. The 1863 passenger list is compiled from two cabin passengers mentioned in a newspaper and Alfred William Craymer's diary of the voyage, so names may be misspelt or completely wrong. I also used the debtors list for the *Gananoque*. It has interesting notes about what the passengers got up to, or what they looked like. It is the only published list for the journey known to exist.

<table>
<tr><td colspan="5" align="center">Passengers 1860[91]</td></tr>
<tr><td colspan="5">Crew</td></tr>
<tr><td>Surname</td><td>Given Name</td><td>Age</td><td>Location</td><td>Occupation/ Notes</td></tr>
<tr><td>Morris</td><td>Archibald</td><td></td><td></td><td>Commander</td></tr>
<tr><td>Brown</td><td>John Ansell</td><td></td><td></td><td>Doctor</td></tr>
<tr><td>Mellars</td><td>George Frederick</td><td></td><td></td><td>Third Mate</td></tr>
<tr><td colspan="5">Chief Cabin</td></tr>
<tr><td>Surname</td><td>Given Name</td><td>Age</td><td>Location</td><td>Occupation/ Notes</td></tr>
<tr><td>Bilton</td><td>Mr. J.</td><td></td><td></td><td></td></tr>
<tr><td>Congreve</td><td>Mr. W.</td><td></td><td></td><td></td></tr>
<tr><td>Ferguson</td><td>Mr. J. D.</td><td></td><td></td><td></td></tr>
<tr><td>Goodrich</td><td>Mr. W. W.</td><td></td><td></td><td></td></tr>
<tr><td>Karslake</td><td>Mr. J. K.</td><td></td><td></td><td></td></tr>
<tr><td>Knyvett</td><td>Mr. C. F.</td><td></td><td></td><td></td></tr>
<tr><td></td><td>Mrs</td><td></td><td></td><td></td></tr>
<tr><td>Knyvett</td><td>Mr. H.</td><td></td><td></td><td></td></tr>
</table>

Surname	Given Name	Age	Location	Occupation/Notes
Lenton	Mr. H.			
Lloyd	Mr. J. H.			
Powell	Mr R.			
Selfe	Mr. J.			
Spooner	Mr. G.			
Sprot	Mr. M.			
Tucker	Mr. E.			
Walker	Mr. W.			
Wilson	Mr. R.			
	Mrs.			
Williams	Mr. H.			
	Mrs			

Second Cabin

Surname	Given Name	Age	Location	Occupation/Notes
Davis	Mr.			
Deresham	Mr.			
Dyer	Mr.			
Hogg	Mr.			
Pinwill	Mr.			
Scully	Mr. W.			
	Mrs.			
	Daughter			
	Son	Infant		*Born on ship*
Woodforde	Mr.			

Paying Steerage

Surname	Given Name	Age	Location	Occupation/Notes
Amor	Richard			
	Mrs.			
Ayres	A. (Aaron)			
	Mrs.			
Cussell	J.			
Denman	J.			

Surname	Given Name	Age	Location	Occupation/Notes
	Mrs.			
Deresham	Mary			
Kirtzell	Charles			
Lorrimer	W.			
Petrie	R.			
	Mrs.			
Pope	F. B.			
Robertson	Jeannie			
Scully	Maria			
Smith	F.			
Stevenson	John			
Stevenson	Sarah	38		*Died on voyage*
Straitton	J.			
Stringer	J.			

Government Immigrants

Married Couples

Surname	*Given Name*	*Age*	*Location*	*Occupation/ Notes*
Binnie	John	36	Lanarkshire	Ploughman
	Elizabeth	24		
Breakwell	John	23	Staffordshire	Farm Labourer
	Ellen	20		
Burrows	Henry	23	Lincolnshire	Farm Labourer
	Elizabeth	23		
	William Henry	5		
Cairncross	Daniel	31	Forfar	Ploughman
	Agnes	27		
	Agnes	8		
	George	5		
	John	3		
	David	1		
Campbell	Arthur	28	Down	Farm Labourer
	Margaret	27		
	Alexander	7		

				Died on the passage from Belfast to Plymouth
	Hannah	5		
Card	William	23	Surrey	Slatter
	Elizabeth	24		
Crooks	Robert	22	Larnarkshire	Gardener
	Elizabeth	28		
Feather	James	35	Yorkshire	Farm Labourer
	Elizabeth	32		
	Edwin	9		
	Emily	6		
	Ann Amelia	2		
Forgan	James	38	Lanarkshire	Labourer
	Isabella	21		
Fuller	Julius	34	Surrey	Miller
	Maria	31		
Gibson	Samuel	23	Down	Farm Labourer
	Martha	25		
Green	Samuel	31	Middlesex	Oilman
	Susan	31		
	Morris Gananoque	Infant		*Born on ship*
Hay	David	26	Forfar	Ploughman
	Margaret	26		
Hughes	Bartholomew Joseph	31	Warwickshire	Carpenter
	Emma	29		
Humm	William	22	Essex	Farm Labourer
	Eliza	20		
	James	2		
	George	Infant		
Kitchingham	Jabez Richard	42	Middlesex	Gardener
	Jane Thomazina	41		
	Emma	11		

	Jane	10		
	Ann	8		
	Eliza	6		
	Sarah	3		
	Henry	1		
Lovsey (Lovesay)	Emma	22	T/F to single women	Travelled with Kitchingham
Newnham	Emma	43	T/F to single women	Travelled with Kitchingham
McKenzie	James	33	Perth	Ploughman
	Elizabeth	33		
	Alexander	11		
	James	9		
Milne	Alexander	23	Aberdeen	Farm Labourer
	Charlotte	28	Kincardine	
	John	3	Kincardine	
	David	Infant	Kincardine	
Peagram	~~Charles~~ John	~~35~~ 28	Essex T/F to single men	Labourer *(see page 22 story)*
	Ann	41		
	Charles	13		
	Edward	11		
	Mary Ann	8		
	Emma	6		
Pepper	Andrew	24	Down	Labourer
	Rachael	23		
	William John	2		
Perrin	John	31		
	Elizabeth	33		
	Joseph Herd	13	T/F to single men	
	William Henry	7		
	John	6		
Robert	William	37	Guernsey	Cabinet Maker
	Lucy Durell	34		

	Lucy	14		
	Angelina	13		
	Walter	10		
	William	6		
	Louisa	2		
Robertson	Duncan	21	Lanarkshire	Ploughman
	Isabella	21		
	John	Infant		
Rosengrave	Thomas	25	Galway	Farm Labourer
	Ann	29		
	Thomas	11		
	Ann	10		
	Eliza	8		
	Jeremiah	7		
	Martin	5		
	Maria	3		
	Margaret	Infant		
Ryan	Thomas	31	Leicestershire	Labourer
	Ann	32		
	Robert	1yr 9 mths		*Died on voyage*
Sands	George William	28	Surrey	Gardener
	Ruth	28		
Sloan	John	27	Down	Farm Labourer
	Catherine	23		
	William	9 mths		
Street	Arthur	23	Middlesex	Carpenter
	Louisa	23		
Thompson	Richard	27	Down	Farm Labourer
	Jane	27		
	Andrew	2 ½		
	William	Infant		

Single Men				
Surname	**Given Name**	**Age**	**Location**	**Occupation/ Notes**
Atkinson	Thomas	22	Yorkshire	Farm Labourer
Brann	John Henry	23	Kent	Schoolmaster on Board Ship
Birnie	James	25	Aberdeen	Farm Labourer
Boycott	William	24	Salop	Miner
Boycott	Richard	20	Salop	Saddler
Cooper	William	27	Down	Farm Labourer
Crampton	George	16	Wicklow	Farm Labourer
Douglas	James	19	Down	Farm Labourer
Gabby	William	21	Down	Farm Labourer
Herd	Joseph	13	Devonshire	
Heron	David	22	Down	Farm Labourer
Heron	John	21	Down	Labourer
Kerr	John	18	Down	Farm Labourer
Kidd	James	54	Perth	Ag. Labourer
Kidd	James	24	Perth	Ag. Labourer
Kidd	Agnes	20	Crossed out	
Kidd	Joshua	17	Perth	Ag. Labourer
Kidd	Elizabeth	12	T/F to single women	
Kidd	Alexander	10		
Leatherdale	George	30	Suffolk	Farm Labourer
Leatherdale	Eliza	18	T/F to single women	
Lomas	John	23	Derby	Farm Labourer
McNiely	Hamilton	21	Down	Farm Labourer
Ogilvie	John	20	Forfar	Joiner
Osborn	David	21	Down	Farm Labourer
Peagram	John	28	Essex	Labourer
Peagram	Charles	13	Essex	
Petrie	Alexander	26	Forfar	Farm Labourer
Shaw	James	30	Down	Blacksmith
Stewart	Archibald	27	Kent	Gardener

Stewart	John	18	Kincardine	Shepherd
Strong	Patrick	24	Tipperary	Farm Labourer
Trail	William	23	Aberdeen	Blacksmith
Tobin	Edward	25	Dublin	Farm Labourer
Tobin	Margaret	23	T/F to single women	(Sister to Edward Tobin)
Tooker	Lawrence	29	King Co.	Farm Labourer
Walls	Francis	23	Aberdeen	Farm Labourer
Wellwood	Joseph	25	King Co.	Farm Labourer

Single Women

Surname	Given Name	Age	Location	Occupation/ Notes
Abeams	Ann	24	Essex	Housemaid
Barrett	Jane	20	Warwick	Domestic Servant
Brown	Sarah Winfield	27	Surrey	Domestic Servant
Canty	Agnes	22	Middlesex	Cook
Dunlop	Jane	28	Down	Factory Girl
Dunlop	Margaret	22	Down	Needlewoman
Gabby	Sabina	23	Down	Needlewoman
Gohey	Mary	18	Gloucestershire	Domestic Servant
Heron	Sarah	20	Down	Domestic Servant
Jenkins	Rosanna	15	Warwickshire	Domestic Servant
Kidd	Elizabeth	12	Perth	
Leatherdale	Eliza	18	Suffolk	Domestic Servant
Lovsey (Lovesay)	Emma	22	Middlesex	Domestic Servant
Macdonald	Sarah	24	King Co.	Domestic Servant
Macdonald	Kate	19	King Co.	Domestic Servant
Martin	Mary	20	Down	Needlewoman
McGee	Catherine	29	Forfar	Dairymaid
McGee	Isabella	18 mths		

Newham	Emma	14	Middlesex	Domestic Servant
Peck	Hannah	28	Essex	
Peck	John Walter	2		
Reddall	Marianne	14	Staf	
Robert	Lucy	14	Guernsey	
Robert	Angelina	13	Guernsey	
Robertson	Jane	24	Perth	Needlewoman
Robertson	Janet	26	Perth	Needlewoman
Robertson	Infant			
Stewart	Mary	24	Kincardine	Dairymaid
Thomson	Isabella	20	Down	Domestic Servant
Tobin	Margaret	23	Dublin	Domestic Servant
Warren	Ellen	27	Middlesex	Nursery Governess
Williams	Emily	26	Kent	Domestic Servant
Worsford	Eliza	29	Surrey	Domestic Servant

Passengers 1861[92]

Crew

Surname	Given Name	Age	Location	Occupation/ Notes
Nixon	William Thomas			Commander
Cridges	Mr.			Ship's Surgeon

Government Immigrants

Steerage

Surname	Given Name	Age	Location	Occupation/ Notes
Boyle	Thos.			(punctuation suggests travel with 2nd John Ryan)
Bruce	Robert			
	Janet			
	Jessie			
Bryce	William			
	Elizabeth			
Buchanan	John			
	Margaret R.			
	Jane			
	Andrew			
Buchanan	Edward			
	Elizabeth			
	Elizabeth			
	Ann			
	James			
	Edward			
	John			
Butcher	William			
Chamberlin	George			

Clark	Jos.			
Coote	Miss.			
Crow	Thos.			
Devine	W.			
	Nicholas			
Eaton	Frederick			
Edmiston	James			
	Catherine			
	Henry			
	Jessie			
Fenton	John			
	Kate			
	Sarah			
Ferguson	Alexander			
Fitzgerald	Martin			Punctuation suggests travel with Walton. W.
Galbraith	David			
Gruther	Robt. M.			
Hall	Mary			
Hall	Thos.			
Hamilton	James			
Hardwood	Isabella			
Hart	Mr.			
Hay	John			
Horner	G.			
Hustwick	Chas.			
Leslie	W.			
Lloyd	Thos.			
	Mrs			
	Lieut			
	Wm.			

	Chas.			
Lodge	William F.			
	Mrs.			
	Elena			
	Kate			
	George			
	Francis			
	Jane			
McAlister	Patrick			
	Agnes			
	Patrick			
	Wm. B.			
	Bethia D.			
	Ellen P.			
	Mary Ann			
	Jessie			
McKay	Wm.			
McNeil	Robt.			
Moylan	Patrick			
	Mary			
Nathan	David			
	Mrs.			
	Miss S.			
	Miss E.			
	Mr Laurence			
Nathan	Lewis			
Newman	Dennis			
	Mary			
North	Chas.			
	M.			
Potts	John			
Rome	George			
Ryan	John (1)			

Ryan	John (2)			Punctuation suggests travel with Boyle T.)
Sinclair	Catherine			
Smellie	Agnes R.			
Somerville	David			
	Christiana			
	Jeanie			
	Henry			
Stack	Lieut.			
Stevens	Andrew			
Stickbury	Jas.			
Stokes	Robt. Y.			
	Margaret			
Swift	John			
	Mary			
Tait	Alex.			
Thompson	Robt.			
Walton	Wm.			Punctuation suggests travel with Fitzgerald M.
Watkins	F.			
Watts	Thos.			
Wells	Abraham			
Wintle	Alfred			
Wylie	W.			
Young	Robt. H.			

Passengers 1863[10]

Crew

Surname	Given Name	Notes
Ritchie	David	Captain
?	?	Second Mate, described as a young lad - had a row with Alfred,
Corse	?	Doctor
Accrington	Mr	A youth who was involved in shaving as they crossed the line. He was probably crew, rather than a passenger
Allen	Jack	Sailor - Sung songs on board and did other antics
?	Boatswain	Had a girl on board who Alfred at one stage thought "would not say boo to a goose"
?	Cook	He was attacked with rheumatism

First Cabin Passengers

Surname	Given Name	Notes
Fraser	Mr	Name from the newspaper report[78]
Fraser	Miss	Name from the newspaper report[78]

Second Cabin and Steerage Passengers

Surname	Given Name	Notes
Caird	Mr George	One night he and his girl were "kissing like fury" much to Alfred's disgust. Later threatened (in fun) to be put in irons for talking to the girls, which was strictly forbidden.
Coleman	Mary	Not mentioned in the diary but mentioned on another website.[84]
Collier	Mr	Thought a pie smelt "hammy" after a ham was stolen and accused a girl. He could be a crew member, but can't confirm this.
Coutts	Janet	Listed[93] as not paying fare of £7
Coutts	Mary	Listed[93] as not paying fare of £7

Craig	Jim (James)	Accused of sending valentines to the cabin passengers
Craig	Andrew	Went up the rigging and was tied up because of it.
Craymer	Alfred William	Writer of the ship's diary aged 23.
Dyson	Elizabeth	Oct 13, 1866 – hadn't paid[93] £3 10
Ellis	Kate	Listed[93] as not paying fare of £7
Ellison	Jane	Listed[93] as not paying fare of £7
Escott	Mr	A young man who attempted to go aloft in the sails of the ship. He also sheared the sheep on board.
Etheridge	Eliza	Listed[93] as not paying fare of £6
Faris	Johnny	Irish lad who had a row with Trustram
Faris	Mary Ann	Listed[93] as not paying fare of £5 10
Farris	Ellen	Listed[93] as not paying fare of £5 10
Fowler	Sarah	Listed[93] as not paying fare of £7
Gaul	Emma	Listed[93] as not paying fare of £7
Gellatly	William	A Scotchman who slept in the same cabin as Craymer and his friends. He had been to America and knew a lot about the war there and sides with the Federals.
Grinean	Mrs or Miss	An eccentric lady who insisted she was Miss not Mrs.
Grinean	Emma	Possibly the same lady as above was listed as not paying fare[93] of £3
Grist	Mrs	Lost her brooch
Haimer	Bridget	July 26, 1871 – hadn't paid[93] £5 10
Hawke	Mr	Suspected of stealing a ham
Hillier	Caroline	Listed[93] as not paying fare of £7
Hogan	Ellen (Helen)	Fell over during bad weather. Listed[93] as not paying fare of £7 10
Hyde	Elizabeth	Listed[93] as not paying fare of £7
Irish Girls		Alfred accused them of stealing jams and preserves from the other girls
Jennings	Ann	Listed[93] as not paying fare of £7

Kelly	Hannah	June 7, 1865 – hadn't paid fare[93] of £5
Kershaw	Betsy	Listed[93] as not paying fare of £8
Lawton	Mr.	Officiated at an English service on board. He was called "Knobs" as he had corns on his feet and his boots were made to accommodate them.
Leebody	Eliza	Listed[93] as not paying fare of £7
Loughlin	Margaret	Listed[93] as not paying fare of £7
Martin	Emma	Listed[93] as not paying fare of £6
Masterton	Elspet	Listed[93] as not paying fare of £6
Mitchell	Mr	Friends with Alfred Craymer, had his 32nd birthday on 21 December 1862
Morgan	Mr	Second Cabin passenger who got very drunk and was lying on the deck. Someone tripped over him and two men tried to throw him overboard but he woke up in time.
Myers	Bridget	Listed[93] as not paying fare of £7
Paterson	Mr	He started a newspaper and they wanted an article from Alfred.
Richmond	Mr. George	He was tied to the main rigging for going up.
Richmond	Mr. (possibly Fred)	A butcher boy
Ryan	Anna	Listed[93] as not paying fare of £6
Savage	Mr.	Wrestled with Watters and won! Wrestled with the Doctor and neither fell. He was called "Coffins" as he had enormous feet and they joked that his boots were big enough to be his coffin!
Smith	Mary Ann	Asked the boatswain to keep a log for her, but Alfred did it instead and wrote an absurd account of the voyage which she probably posted home. Listed[93] as not paying fare of £7
Stevenson	Margaret	Listed[93] as not paying fare of £5

Stewart	Mr	Involved in some story about blue elephants that is hard to understand.
Stott	Mr (Joseph Ebenezer)	Danced with Alice Wade and the Doctor couldn't talk to her and ended up going to bed quite sadly. Later on in the voyage Alfred observed that Mr Stott had fallen "head over heels" for Alice Wade.
Taylor	Jessie	Rolled down the poop ladder during bad weather
Trustrum	Mr.	Left his wife in Great Britain and went to NZ with his 3 daughters and one son all of whom are assisted. He was possibly sent out by the Parish, having "sponged on them long enough". Listed[93] as not paying fare of £4
Trustrum	Emily, Alice and Henrietta	Most likely the daughters of the above Mr Trustrum.[93] March 2, 1870 hadn't paid fares of £13
Trustrum	Edward	Listed[93] as not paying fare of £4. Whether this is Mr Trustrum's son or Mr Trustrum himself cannot be proven.
Wade	Alice	The Doctor had the hots for her. They sat together at a service and seemed very pleased in each other's company. Then Mr. Stott took over!
Watters	Mr	Friends with Alfred Craymer
Welsh	Maggie	An Irish girl with a strong accent and "carroty hair." A girl named Maggie had a water fight with Watters and made the deck wet and Alfred slipped on it. Margaret Welsh[93] was listed as not paying fare of £6.
West	Mr.	Fainted and was treated by Dr Corse.

References

1. Government of Canada, C. H. Ship Information Database. (1996). at <http://www.pro.rcip-chin.gc.ca/bd-dl/nav-ship-eng.jsp?emu=en.vessel:/Proxapp/ws/vessel/public/owners/ResultSetExpanded&&w=NATIVE(%27OFFICIAL_NO+%3D+%27%2733377%27%27%27)&upp=0&rpp=10>

2. Wikipedia contributors. Davie Shipbuilding. *Wikipedia, the free encyclopedia* (2012). at <http://en.wikipedia.org/w/index.php?title=Davie_Shipbuilding&oldid=498358999>

3. DAVIE, GEORGE TAYLOR - Dictionary of Canadian Biography Online. at <http://www.biographi.ca/009004-119.01-e.php?BioId=40785&query=>

4. Siam.jpg (JPEG Image, 428×312 pixels). at <http://www.angelfire.com/az2/ships/images/Siam.jpg>

5. Lloyd's Register of Shipping. *Books Boxes & Boats maritimearchives.co.uk* at <http://www.maritimearchives.co.uk/lloyds-register.html>

6. What is a Clipper Ship? | Marine Insight. at <http://www.marineinsight.com/marine/life-at-sea/maritime-history/what-is-a-clipper-ship-2/>

7. Gananoque Its many spellings Thousand Islands Ontario Canada! at <http://www.gananoque.com/spelling.html>

8. Wikipedia contributors. Gananoque. *Wikipedia, the free encyclopedia* (2012). at <http://en.wikipedia.org/w/index.php?title=Gananoque&oldid=490012401>

9. Taupiri | NZETC - Mellars. at <http://nzetc.victoria.ac.nz/tm/scholarly/tei-Cyc02Cycl-t1-body1-d3-d3-d6.html>

10. Craymer, Alfred William, 1862-1863 Diary of a voyage from England to New Zealand, 5 Dec 1862 - 13 Mar 1863. Alexander Turnbull Library, Reference qMS-0585.

11. Mrs. Margaret Campbell. Gallant Oak. 12 November 1914. *Press* 9 (1914).

12. Lloyd's Register of Shipping - Books Boxes & Boats maritimearchives.co.uk. at <http://www.maritimearchives.co.uk/lloyds-register.html>

13. Haws, Duncan. Shaw, Savill & Albion. at <http://www.merchantnavyofficers.com/shawsavill.html>

14. Wikipedia contributors. Packet ship. *Wikipedia, the free encyclopedia* (2012). at <http://en.wikipedia.org/w/index.php?title=Packet_ship&oldid=481049374>

15. Taonga, N. Z. M. for C. and H. T. M. Settlement in the provinces: 1853 to 1870. at <http://www.teara.govt.nz/en/history-of-immigration/5>

16. Acland, J. B. A. Shipping papers 'Clontarf, A1': ships regulations and plan. University of Canterbury. Acland. (1855).

17. Shaw, Savill And Albion Company | NZETC. at <http://nzetc.victoria.ac.nz/tm/scholarly/tei-Bre01Whit-t1-body-d5.html>

18. Costs and Wages in Great Britain. at <http://www.rootsweb.ancestry.com/~irlcar2/wages.htm>

19. Purdy, F. On the Earnings of Agricultural Labourers in England and Wales, 1860. *Journal of the Statistical Society of London* **24,** 328–373 (1861).

20. Life at Sea: Museum Victoria. at <http://museumvictoria.com.au/discoverycentre/websites-mini/journeys-australia/1850s70s/life-at-sea/>

21. Diver, M. *The Voyages of the Clontarf.* (Dornie Publishing Company, 2011).

22. SHIPPING INTELLIGENCE. HOBSON'S BAY. 18 November 1858. *The Argus* 4 (1858).

23. SHIPPING INTELLIGENCE. HOBSON'S BAY. 26 November 1858. *The Argus* 4 (1858).

24. COMMERCIAL INTELLIGENCE. The Argus Office, Wednesday Evening. - Mail for Mauritius. 27 January 1859. *The Argus* 4 (1859).

25. Page 1 Advertisements Column 1. 28 June 1870. *Colonist* 1 (1870).

26. DATABASE OF SHIP COLLISIONS WITH ICEBERGS. at <http://researchers.imd.nrc.ca/~hillb/icedb/ice/bergs2_01e.html#G>

27. Gananoque1860. at <http://freepages.genealogy.rootsweb.ancestry.com/~ourstuff/Gananoque.htm>

28. View Images — FamilySearch.org - Passenger List Chrysolite 1861. at <https://familysearch.org/pal:/MM9.3.1/TH-267-11661-100939-67?cc=1609792&wc=MMBG-R3Y:1030761315>

29. Tristan da Cunha. *Wikipedia, the free encyclopedia* (2012). at <http://en.wikipedia.org/w/index.php?title=Tristan_da_Cunha&oldid=520770805>

30. Acclimatisation. Skylarks on Gananoque 17 August 1861. *Press* 1 (1861).
31. Shipping News. Arrival of Gananoque 1860. 12 May 1860. *Lyttelton Times* 4 (1860).
32. Miss Rye's-emigrants. Discussion on female immigration. 12 September 1863. *Daily Southern Cross* 4 (1863).
33. The Gananoque | NZETC - 1860 journey. at <http://nzetc.victoria.ac.nz/tm/scholarly/tei-Bre01Whit-t1-body-d71.html>
34. Racing Men I Have Known - 27 July 1892. *Press* 2 (1892).
35. Papers Past — Lyttelton Times — 28 January 1860 — Shipping News. at <http://paperspast.natlib.govt.nz/cgi-bin/paperspast?a=d&cl=search&d=LT18600128.2.6&srpos=1&e=28-01-1860-28-01-1860--10-LT-1----0butler-->
36. Reminiscences Of Canterbury In 1860. 24 December 1892. *Press* 2 (1892).
37. Shipping News. - Gananoque sails for Callao. 25 July 1860. *Lyttelton Times* 4 (1860).
38. Callao To Valparaiso. 10 January 1871. *North Otago Times* 2 (1871).
39. RootsWeb: GENANZ-L Richard Prince Amor's Daughter. at <http://listsearches.rootsweb.com/th/read/GENANZ/1996-11/0847154672>
40. Mr. Aaron Ayers | NZETC. at <http://nzetc.victoria.ac.nz/tm/scholarly/tei-Cyc03Cycl-t1-body1-d3-d9-d15.html>
41. Farmers, Old Settlers, Etc | NZETC - John Henry Charles Brann. at <http://nzetc.victoria.ac.nz/tm/scholarly/tei-Cyc01Cycl-t1-body-d4-d172-d26.html#name-415947-mention>
42. Funeral Notice. Lucy Martha Brann. 4 November 1902. *Wanganui Chronicle* 4 (1902).
43. Breakwell - Breakwell - Family History & Genealogy Message Board - Ancestry.ca. at <http://boards.ancestry.ca/surnames.breakwell/1/mb.ashx>
44. *Christchurch Parish Records. Peterborough Central Library, Christchurch.*
45. District Court. John Breakwell, bankruptcy. 16 July 1875. *Timaru Herald* 3 (1875).
46. Great Grandma's Wicker Basket: The Meng Children's Stepmother - Sarah Winfield Brown. at <http://greatgrandmaswickerbasket.blogspot.co.nz/2012/05/meng-childrens-stepmother.html>
47. [Cheviot and McKenzie] | NZETC George William Crampton. at <http://nzetc.victoria.ac.nz/tm/scholarly/tei-Cyc03Cycl-t1-body1-d4-d36-d1.html>
48. Obituary. - Green. 7 December 1904. *Star* 3 (1904).
49. Waddington | NZETC - William Humm. at <http://nzetc.victoria.ac.nz/tm/scholarly/tei-Cyc03Cycl-t1-body1-d6-d39.html>
50. John Karslake Karslake. *Wikipedia, the free encyclopedia* (2012). at <http://en.wikipedia.org/w/index.php?title=John_Karslake_Karslake&oldid=482518500>
51. Farmers | NZETC Joshua Kidd. at <http://nzetc.victoria.ac.nz/tm/scholarly/tei-Cyc03Cycl-t1-body1-d4-d29-d2.html>
52. Personal Items. - Jackson. 12 August 1924. *Hawera & Normanby Star* 4 (1924).
53. George Frederick **MELLARS** + Mary Rose **GIBBS** - TAUPIRI, Waikato :: FamilyTreeCircles.com Genealogy. at <http://www.familytreecircles.com/george-frederick-mellars-mary-rose-gibbs-taupiri-1863-47701.html>
54. Petane | NZETC - David Milne. at <http://nzetc.victoria.ac.nz/tm/scholarly/tei-Cyc06Cycl-t1-body1-d2-d25-d1.html#Cyc06Cycl-fig-Cyc06Cycl413b>
55. Here And There. 10 December 1930. *Evening Post* 15 (1930).
56. Castle Eden arrived Lyttelton 1851. at <http://freepages.genealogy.rootsweb.ancestry.com/~nzbound/castleeden.htm>
57. News Of The Day. 11 January 1927. *Evening Post* 6 (1927).
58. Pioneer Gathering. 17 December 1907. *Press* 6 (1907).
59. Christchurch. Andrew Pepper drowning. 14 September 1861. *Press* 5 (1861).
60. Town and Country News. Andrew Pepper drowning. 11 September 1861. *Lyttelton Times* 4 (1861).
61. Women's Corner. Mrs Goggin. 12 May 1920. *Press* 2 (1920).
62. Birth, Death and Marriage Historical Records. at <https://bdmhistoricalrecords.dia.govt.nz/Home/>
63. Deaths. Arthur Street. 30 May 1865. *Lyttelton Times* 5 (1865).
64. Arthur and Louisa Street emigrated from London UK, and their children Louisa, Harry and Frank, Lyttelton NZ 1860's-looking for departure of sons to NSW AUS c.1893-1901 :: FamilyTreeCircles.com Genealogy. at <http://www.familytreecircles.com/arthur-and-louisa-

street-emigrated-from-london-uk-and-their-children-louisa-harry-and-frank-lyttelton-nz-1860-s-looking-for-departure-of-sons-to-nsw-a-50951.html>

65. Obituary. Mr Joseph Henry Stringer. 19 October 1920. *Press* 7 (1920).

66. Inberhuny? - General - Family History & Genealogy Message Board - Ancestry.com. at <http://boards.ancestry.com/localities.britisles.ireland.dow.general/267.1.1/mb.ashx>

67. Farmers | NZETC William John Thompson. at <http://nzetc.victoria.ac.nz/tm/scholarly/tei-Cyc03Cycl-t1-body1-d4-d15-d2.html>

68. Gananoque 1861 journey. at <http://freepages.genealogy.rootsweb.ancestry.com/~shipstonz/PassLists/gananoque1861.html>

69. Shipping Intelligence. Arrival of the Gananoque to Auckland 1861. 15 November 1861. *Wellington Independent* 2 (1861).

70. Captain Kynaston's patented slip or disengaging hook for lowering boats. at <http://www.pdavis.nl/Kynaston.php>

71. News Of The Day. 17 October 1931. *Auckland Star* 8 (1931).

72. The Gananoque. 23 August 1924. *Auckland Star* 17 (1924).

73. Commercial Summary. Gananoque Cargo 1861. 5 November 1861. *Daily Southern Cross* 2 3 (1861).

74. Obituary. - Buchanan. 2 October 1931. *Auckland Star* 3 (1931).

75. Personal. - Edmiston. 23 January 1912. *Auckland Star* 5 (1912).

76. Nathan, L. D. and Co | NZETC. at <http://nzetc.victoria.ac.nz/tm/scholarly/tei-Cyc02Cycl-t1-body1-d1-d52-d17.html>

77. Mr James Stichbury. 25 April 1903. *Observer* 20 (1903).

78. Shipping Intelligence. - Gananoque journey to Otago arrival 1863. 13 March 1863. *Otago Daily Times* 4 (1863).

79. News Of The Week. Joseph Stott leaving colony. 21 July 1865. *Otago Witness* 11 12,13 (1865).

80. Papers Past — Otago Daily Times — 4 May 1863 — DEPARTURES. at <http://paperspast.natlib.govt.nz/cgi-bin/paperspast?a=d&cl=search&d=ODT18630504.2.8&srpos=1&e=-------10--1----0%22Gananoque%2c+ship%2c+785+tons%2c+Rifchie%2c+for+Guam%2c+in+ballast%22-->

81. [General] | NZETC George Caird. at <http://nzetc.victoria.ac.nz/tm/scholarly/tei-Cyc01Cycl-t1-body-d4-d134-d3.html>

82. Family Tree Maker's Genealogy Site: User Home Page Book: Marshall Family History: Register Report of Thomas McDonald. at <http://familytreemaker.genealogy.com/users/m/a/r/Paul-I-Marshall-Bucks/BOOK-0001/0006-0004.html>

83. they lost their lives on the SS WAIRARAPA - midnight 28 October 1894 :: FamilyTreeCircles.com Genealogy. at <http://www.familytreecircles.com/ss-wairarapa-25770.html>

84. Wairaprapra1894 - Mary Coleman. at <http://freepages.genealogy.rootsweb.ancestry.com/~ourstuff/SSWairarapaPass.htm>

85. Scotts in Banff & Moray - General - Family History & Genealogy Message Board - Ancestry.co.uk. at <http://boards.ancestry.co.uk/thread.aspx?mv=flat&m=925&p=localities.britisles.scotland.ban.general>

86. Shipping Summary. Cargo on Gananoque 1864. 17 September 1864. *Southland Times* 4 (1864).

87. Port Of Bluff Harbor. - Arrival of Gananoque to Southland 1864. 6 September 1864. *Southland Times* 2 (1864).

88. Resident Magistrate's Court Campbelltown. 22 October 1864. *Southland Times* 3 (1864).

89. Papers Past — Southland Times — 2 November 1864 — PORT OF BLUFF HARBOR. at <http://paperspast.natlib.govt.nz/cgi-bin/paperspast?a=d&d=ST18641102.2.3.4&cl=search&srpos=15&e=-------10--1----0gananoque-->

90. Nicholson, I. *Log of Logs - Vol. 2, page 197.*

91. View Images — FamilySearch.org - Gananoque Passenger List 1860. at <https://familysearch.org/pal:/MM9.3.1/TH-266-11580-41390-27?cc=1609792&wc=MMBP-HHL:1784627422>

92. Port Of Raglan. Arrival of Gananoque to Auckland 1861. 22 October 1861. *Daily Southern Cross* 3 (1861).

93. List of Immigrants, Debtors to the Provincial Government of Otago for Passage Moneys, 1872 -

(Covers 1856-1872) - Photocopy [use REPRO 1716] (R21580774). Agency ACHU. Series, 19316. Record Group, MISC43a. Box/Item, 1/. Archives New Zealand, Wellington Office.